ANCIENT SOUTH AMERICA

Recent Evidence Supporting Edgar Cayce's Story of Atlantis and Mu

Gregory L. Little, Ed. D.
John Van Auken
Lora Little, Ed. D.

Eagle Wing Books, Inc.
Memphis, Tennessee

Ancient South America

Copyright © 2002
        by Greg Little, John Van Auken, and Lora Little

Hand Illustrations © 2002 by Dee Turman

Published by
        Eagle Wing Books, Inc.
        P. O. Box 9972
        Memphis, TN 38190

web sites:
        www.eaglewingbooks.com
        www.mysterious-america.net
        www.edgarcayce.org/am
        www.yucatanhallofrecords.com

ISBN: 0940829355
Retail Price: $8.95
First U.S.A. Printing: August 2002

Table of Contents

SOUTH AMERICA

HONDURAS
Tegucigalpa
NICARAGUA
Managua
COSTA RICA
San José
Panama
PANAMA

Caribbean Sea

Isla de
San Andrés
(COLOMBIA)

Barranquilla
Cartagena
Maracaibo
Barquisimeto
Cúcuta
San Cristóbal

Martinique (FRANCE)
ST. LUCIA
Aruba Netherlands ST. VINCENT AND
(NETH.) Antilles THE GRENADINES
(NETH.) GRENADA

BARBADOS

Caracas
Valencia
TRINIDAD AND
TOBAGO
Port-of-Spain

Isla de Malpelo
(COLOMBIA)

Medellín
Bogotá
Cali
COLOMBIA

Ciudad
Guayana
VENEZUELA
Boa Vista

Georgetown
GUYANA
Paramaribo
SURINAME
Cayenne
French
Guiana
(FRANCE)

GUIANA HIGHLANDS

North
Atlantic
Ocean

Equator

Quito
ECUADOR
Guayaquil

A M A Z O N

Macapá

Iquitos

Piura

PERU
Lima

Trujillo

South
Pacific
Ocean

Huánuco

B A S I N

Rio
Branco

Pôrto
Velho

Cuzco

ANDES

Arequipa

Arica

Iquique

ALTIPLANO

La Paz
BOLIVIA
Cochabamba Santa Cruz
Sucre
Potosí

Manaus

Santarém

Belém

Manaus

MATO GROSSO
PLATEAU

Cuiabá

BRAZIL

Brasília
Goiânia

Uberlândia

São Luís

Fortaleza

Teresina

Natal

Recife

Maceió

Salvador

BRAZILIAN

HIGHLANDS

Belo
Horizonte

Tropic of Capricorn

Isla San Félix
(CHILE)

Antofagasta

Isla San Ambrosio
(CHILE)

ARCHIPIÉLAGO
JUAN FERNÁNDEZ
(CHILE)

ATACAMA DESERT

Salta

CHILE

Cerro Aconcagua
(highest point in
South America, 6962 m)

Valparaíso
Santiago

Concepción

San Miguel
de Tucumán

Resistencia

PARAGUAY

Asunción

Campo
Grande

Rio de Janeiro
São Paulo
Santos
Curitiba

Florianópolis

Vitória

Pôrto Alegre

Córdoba Santa Fe
Mendoza Rosario
La Plata
Buenos Aires

Salto
URUGUAY

South
Atlantic
Ocean

ANDES

PAMPAS

ARGENTINA

Bahía Blanca

Montevideo

Mar del Plata

Puerto Montt

San Carlos de
Bariloche

PATAGONIA

Península Valdés
(lowest point in
South America, -40 m)

Comodoro Rivadavia

Scale 1:35,000,000
Azimuthal Equal-Area Projection

0   500 Kilometers
0   500 Miles

Boundary representation is
not necessarily authoritative.

Río
Gallegos

Punta Arenas

Strait of
Magellan

Ushuaia

Stanley
Falkland Islands
(Islas Malvinas)
(administered by U.K.,
claimed by ARGENTINA)

South Georgia and the
South Sandwich Islands
(administered by U.K.,
claimed by ARGENTINA)

802634AI (R02108) 6-99

Chapter 1

Introduction

The South American Archaeology Problem: North American Archaeologists *versus* South American Archaeologists

The ancient history of South America is perhaps more mysterious and enigmatic than any other area of the world. There are a host of reasons for this, but the reality is that, other than a familiarity with the Inca citadels in the Andes, Americans know little about the fascinating ancient sites in South America. The impact made on the continent by 15th-century European conquerors and treasure seekers nearly wiped clean the collective memory of the many indigenous people already living in the land. In addition, in virtually every region of South America, there are legends telling of a great flood that killed nearly all of the ancient people who lived there. The legends tell that after this flood, a small group of survivors restarted civilization in the region. These mythical people were eventually joined by others who entered South America from unknown places. A later chapter will summarize these legends. Finally, a host of evidence shows that at various times in the remote past, the different groups of people who migrated into South America caused conflicts leading to major reductions in population centers and the complete destruction of cultures. All of these factors appear to contribute to a lack of understanding about ancient South America.

Most Americans believe that ancient South America was almost completely uninhabited in ancient times, but that is not the case. According to South American archaeologists,[1] the population of South

America was between 30 million and 84 million in 1492. These people—and their ancestors—left behind an amazing legacy that is only now becoming fully appreciated outside the region.

The North American Archaeology Belief System

South American archaeology has long been dominated by American academic archaeologists, and research there has been both facilitated and hampered by this factor. For the past 70 years, American archaeology has been driven by the idea that the Americas were virtually uninhabited prior to *circa* 9500 B.C. This belief, long presented as an indisputable fact in many textbooks, insisted that **all** the people who entered ancient America came across the Bering Strait from Siberia during the last Ice Age. These people, termed *Clovis* by archaeologists, supposedly entered in a single migrational wave in about 9500 B.C. and quickly populated all of the Americas. The idea also asserted that North America was inhabited *before* South America. The theory proposed that all of the Native Americans—both North and South Americans—were racially or genetically related.

Most American archaeologists consistently and vehemently rejected any suggestions that anyone else entered the Americas between approximately 9500 B.C. and A.D. 1492. Gustavo Politis, a Brazilian archaeologist and university professor, wrote in 1999 that "the hundreds of North American archaeologists" working in South America do not "share the cultural idiosyncrasies" of South America. In addition, Politis asserts that the tradition of research is vastly different between the two regions, and that "the perception of reality is different."[2] In brief, North American archaeologists have consistently dismissed the many South American finds indicating human occupation prior to the Clovis-first Barrier (9500 B.C.) as poorly conducted or contaminated research. The dominant American perception of reality was simple: no one *could* have been in South America prior to 9500 B.C. Thus, driven by this "idea as a fact," the reasoning was simple: all evidence that emerged contradicting that belief simply had to be faulty. Politis is blunt in his assessment of the belief-driven American archaeologists: "The region seems to have been used as a source both of raw data and of social and political 'Edens' or imaginary laboratories of social processes with which to back up Euro-American archaeological theories or political agendas." South American archaeologists have long had the perception that their northern counterparts were driven by a belief of supremacy and scientific superiority, causing a perceptual bias that saw South American science as inferior.

In fairness, some American archaeologists have hedged a bit on possible migrations to the Americas prior to the Clovis-first Barrier, but only because Americans were involved in the studies proposing the idea. In his scathing but often glaringly inaccurate attack on all ideas outside the American academic mainstream, Stephen Williams[3] relates that the fact that the Clovis people inhabited all the Americas so quickly is notable. There is "reasonable speculation," as he describes it, that someone could have entered South America before Clovis. If it were true, Williams sarcastically adds, "these ancient travelers probably did not know the magnitude of their own accomplishment." Such speculation by American academics, however, is almost always based on the assumption that the people arriving in South America in very early times came from the north—by staying on the Pacific coastline of America before "eventually" settling in the south. The "we were first" theory still holds sway in American academic thinking.

More representative of academic archaeological beliefs are the textbooks utilized in college classes. For example, in *Kentucky Archaeology* (1996), Tankersley writes: "The first people to inhabit Kentucky were the hunters and gatherers who lived at the end of the last Ice Age (approx. 9500 to 8000 B.C.)."[4] *The Encyclopedia Smithsonian* states it bluntly: "The traditional theory held that the first Americans crossed the land bridge from Siberia to Alaska around 11,500 years ago." James Adovasio, Director of the Mercyhurst Archaeological Institute, termed the Clovis-first idea the *holy writ* of American archaeology, and that even suggesting it was wrong was a "heresy." Grants, academic jobs, and publishing in the tightly controlled journals all depended on adherence to the Clovis-first belief.

The Clovis-first belief was not shared by archaeologists from South America or those in other parts of the world. The French text, *The World Atlas of Archaeology* (1985),[5] acknowledges the Americans' view (9500 B.C. as the earliest possible date of human occupation) but flatly states that discoveries favor the idea that South America was inhabited before 30,000 B.C. For example, a host of Brazilian archaeologists have found reliable evidence of human occupation at several sites in that country ranging from 50,000 B.C. to as early as 300,000 B.C.[2]

Clovis-First Collapses

It is fitting that excavations conducted at a South American site collapsed the Clovis-first barrier, ultimately sending American academic archaeologists into a needed turmoil and reevaluation. But only Americans were able to do so. In the 1980s a team of archaeologists from the University of Kentucky began conducting regular excavations at a site in southern Chile. The site, called Monte Verde, had a layer of Clovis artifacts, but the researchers had found layers of human habitation below the Clovis layer. After almost two decades of debate, in 1997 a "blue-ribbon panel" of 12 American archaeologists, including skeptics and Clovis-first proponents, was dispatched to assess the Monte Verde evidence. All 12 members agreed that Monte Verde had been occupied 1000 years prior to Clovis. On the day the panel made their much-publicized announcement, an even deeper layer of artifacts was uncovered dating from 33,000 to 37,000 years ago. This stunning discovery curiously caused a few on the panel to later state that something had to be wrong at Monte Verde, because Clovis was first. But many American archaeologists subsequently returned to sites in North America where they had previously uncovered Clovis artifacts and dug deeper. Much to their surprise, a host of sites showed human occupation thousands of years before Clovis. The reason that the deeper layers of occupation hadn't been uncovered by the previous excavations was simple. In the past, digging stopped when Clovis was found, because "there couldn't be anything else there."

During this same time period, other evidence from archaeological digs emerged. In Brazil a skull found at Serra Da Capivara was dated to 50,000 B.C. Across the world cocaine and nicotine were discovered in a host of mummies from Egypt, Germany, and the Sudan. Since tobacco and the coca plant are known to have been present only in the Americas, the implication was that some sort of trading system existed in ancient times.

Much to the chagrin of traditional American archaeology, the 1990s also saw genetic and viral data emerge that completely collapsed all the prevailing views of the ancient past. In Japan researchers investigating a highly specific type of leukemia virus found it to be present in only two groups: the Atacamanian people of Japan and in 1500-year-old mummies recovered from the Andes Mountains of Chile. The researchers concluded that 25,000 years ago a small group of the Atacamanian people migrated to South America. In addition, another line of genetic research has been conducted, starting in the late 1980s. This type of genetic testing (called mitochondrial DNA, or **mtDNA**) can identify the maternal lineage of a living individual or of human remains as well as determine the time the individual's ancestors migrated from their land of origin. (More on the significance of this research and how it is conducted will come later.)

Many American archaeologists still argue for a single migration from Siberia and insist that these ancient people all came "down" from the north. The mtDNA research in North America, however, has shown three probable migrations. The first occurred about 47,000-33,000 years ago. The second occurred in 28,000 B.C. The third occurred in 10,000 B.C. These people came from Siberia, China, Japan, and the South Pacific. However, a mysterious type of mtDNA, called haplogroup X, came into America several times from an "unknown" location. These people entered America before 33,000 B.C.; also in 28,000 B.C.; and again in 10,000 B.C. Haplogroup X has sometimes been inaccurately portrayed as "European" in origin, but its origin is unknown, and it does not necessarily represent "white" or "Caucasian" races. The book *Mound Builders*[6] by the present authors extensively presents all this data.

In addition to the ancient migrational waves to the Americas as indicated by the mtDNA research, another curious finding has emerged. Parts of the Americas appear to have been inhabited by humans *before* any of these migrations took place. This is accepted as fact by most South American researchers but is rejected as fantasy by their northern counterparts.

The vast majority of those who read this small book will be in North America and will probably find the overview of South American archaeological discoveries to be completely unexpected. What must be kept in mind is that the media in North America almost exclusively focuses on the "scientific pronouncements" made by North Americans. Thus many of the discoveries made in South America by Latin American archaeologists have literally been ignored or vehemently ridiculed as flawed and inferior science. This does not appear to be the reality, however, and a mass of reliable, rigorous scientific research indicates that the South American archaeologists have been correct. In the scientific field much has been at stake in this debate, but the primary "prizes" clearly seem to be pride, ego, feelings of superiority, and the proliferation of statements in support of specific beliefs usually cast as indisputable facts. In a very real sense, there is a background of interpersonal psychological and social factors at work in archaeology that has created perceptual bias. The most frequent mechanism of reasoning employed in such bias is represented in a simple sentence: "It can't be true; therefore, it isn't." Such reasoning is often used to criticize archaeological research that appears to show the long-held dogmatic beliefs to be false.

The Edgar Cayce Enigma

The mere mention of America's famous "Sleeping Prophet," Edgar Cayce, in a book on South American prehistory and archaeology probably strikes most readers as odd or perhaps even cultish. Cayce (*b.* 1877; *d.* 1945) is often considered to be the "Father of the Holistic Health Movement," a result of substantial medical research on the health readings he gave while in a self-induced trance state for thousands of individuals. Over the more than 40 years that Cayce gave readings, a total of 14,256 documented readings were given to over 6000 people. About 68 percent of his readings were health-related, but in the early 1920s a new type of reading emerged, when an individual began questioning the entranced Cayce about more philosophical issues. Cayce was unaware of what had transpired during his readings, and a stenographer had to read to him what "he" had said during the trance state in response to questions. What emerged during this particular set of questions shocked Cayce and nearly led him to completely abandon the practice.

The reading related that humans typically led many lives on earth and that in a very real way the present life of an individual was influenced by what the individual had done in past lives. As a deeply religious and devout Christian, this information shocked him and led to great doubts. But so many people had been helped by the health readings that Cayce and his family decided to continue requested readings with a simple understanding. If anyone were ever hurt by a reading, he would stop. But no one was ever hurt by his readings, so they continued until his death in 1945.

Cayce came to accept the information on past lives, but he saw it as "The Continuity of Life" rather than a belief in reincarnation. The readings on past lives came to be termed *Life Readings* and have become the focal point of much speculation and public anticipation in archaeological discoveries. For example, it is probably true that most Americans have heard that there is a chamber under the Sphinx at Giza in Egypt, and that in this chamber are ancient historical records. This idea emerged from Cayce's readings. A host of other specific statements about the ancient past came from Cayce's readings and have been found to be true.

It must be emphasized that Cayce was not infallible—nor did he ever claim to be. In particular, two types of Cayce's readings appear to be inaccurate. Readings in which individuals were seeking unearned wealth by digging up buried treasure, gold, or oil invariably failed. In addition, *some* of what are popularly characterized as his "psychic prediction readings"—predictions about specific future events—are questionable. However, nearly always ignored in this debate is the fact that Cayce stated numerous times that the future is not set and that people can change outcomes.

Cayce's Visions of the Ancient World

The third of Cayce's readings that are not health readings are mostly life readings, containing information about the past lives of various individuals. Over the decades, a consistent picture of the ancient world emerged from bits and pieces cumulated from these life readings. For example, Cayce related in 1925[7] that the first "human-like" beings emerged on earth about 10 million years ago. In 1925, scientists believed that human-like creatures had been around for perhaps 200,000 years.[8] Interestingly, in July of 2002 the journal *Nature* reported that the oldest known skull of a hominid (humankind's earliest known relative) had been found in Chad. It has been dated as 7-8 million years old.

The Cayce readings make it clear that parts of North and South America were inhabited well before 50,000 B.C. Cayce also related that a South Pacific Continent called Mu had existed, and that some of its people migrated to South America and North America at quite specific times (for example, 50,000 B.C. and 28,000 B.C.). He also stated that Atlantis had existed close to the Caribbean Ocean and sank *circa* 10,000 B.C. Atlanteans had migrated to America, Central and South America, several places in Europe, the Middle East, and to the Gobi in 50,000 B.C., 28,000 B.C., and 10,000 B.C. In *Mound Builders*[6] we examined 68 Cayce readings on ancient America, especially focusing on what his readings had related about this mysterious culture. When he began these readings (in 1923), everything he stated about ancient America was completely and diametrically opposed to archaeological belief. With the collapse of the Clovis-first barrier in 1997 and the new genetic research emerging, we decided to compare Cayce's statements to the new scientific information. What resulted was astounding: 77 percent of his impossible ideas were supported by scientific evidence; 20 percent could neither be verified nor discounted because of insufficient evidence; and only 3 percent appeared inaccurate. The single inaccurate reading was one in which an individual was seeking confirmation of her belief that she had been related to a famous person. Interestingly, in several readings Cayce related that the ego desires of individuals seeking readings could influence the information, causing it to be inaccurate. More detailed information on Cayce's ancient history can be found in *Mound Builders*[6] and the 2000 book, *The Lost Hall of Records.*[9]

Our Purpose

This book is *not* intended to be an exhaustive review of South American archaeology or an exhaustive review of Cayce. Instead, our goal is to first present an overview of some of the important discoveries and archaeological eras that have been identified in ancient South America to acquaint the reader with the rich heritage of this land. In addition, a summary of the newest genetic evidence will be outlined, along with a simple explanation of the South American migrations that probably occurred in ancient times. A summary of mythology from various areas of South America will be included with brief comparisons to other cultures. Finally, we will review Cayce's major statements about South America and compare them with the current scientific evidence.

Chapter 2

Overview of South America's Ancient Past

As stated in Chapter One, some South American archaeologists have dated the earliest known habitation on the continent at 300,000 B.C.[1] Of course, that date has been ridiculed and ignored by American archaeologists who stuck to the 9500-B.C. date as the first possible entry of humans into the Americas—at least until 1997. What is quite interesting in this ongoing debate is that Americans have also ignored the *Radiocarbon Database for the Andes,*[2] which lists 87 different human habitation sites in the Andes region alone that predate Clovis. Most of these pre-Clovis dates were published prior to 1997. The 87 pre-Clovis dates range from 46,800 B.C. to 10,000 B.C. Nine test sites carbon dated to *before* 40,000 B.C., and another 33 dated to between 40,000 B.C. and 30,000 B.C. In a 2000 book chapter titled, "The Original Peopling of Latin America," Bryan writes, "Significant differences between the archaeology of North and South America now become evident. North American archaeologists looking for cultural origins naturally look back to Beringia and Siberia."[3] It has been inconceivable to American archaeologists that anyone else could have entered America before 9500 B.C. Perhaps even more biased is the Americans' belief that North America had to be settled before South America.

The Earliest Habitation: Evidence From Excavations

In 1986, archaeologist Maria Beltrao was excavating a cave named Toca da Esperança (Grotto of Hope) in central Brazil. She found

SOUTH AMERICA

the bones of an extinct horse and a stone implement. The bones showed definite signs of being cut by the implement, indicating that the horse had been butchered by humans. Because radiocarbon dating can only test reliably to approximately 50,000 years ago, the bones were sent to a radiation laboratory in France for the more sensitive uraniumthorium dating method. In 1986 the results of the testing were announced. The horse had been killed 300,000 years ago.[1, 3] At the time, American archaeologists either ignored the results or scorned them as being obviously tainted. For example Americans cited 45,000 B.C. radiocarbon dates obtained at the site obviously ignoring the limits of radiocarbon methods. At the same time, archaeologists discovered fascinating paintings in a nearby cave called the Grotto of the Cosmos. Suns, stars, and comets were depicted in the cave, which was then dated to over 10,000 years old. One red comet was depicted with an almost five-foot-long tail against a backdrop of stars.

The controversy at Toca da Esperança is similar to one ignited by a find at Hueyatlaco near Valsequillo, Mexico. In the 1960s two Mexican archaeologists found stone tools at several sites located about 75 miles southeast of Mexico City. A team of geologists from the U.S. Geological Survey used four methods to date the layer containing the tools (including uranium series dating, fission track dating, and tephra hydrating dating). The site had been occupied in 250,000 B.C. The results were published in a 1981 issue of *Quaternary Research*, and were immediately assailed by American archaeologists.

Extremely ancient cave paintings and rock art are found the entire length of South America. In the Brazil state of Piauí a huge rock shelter named Pedra Furada is covered with ancient paintings. In 1983, radiocarbon testing dated one of the layers of habitation to about 24,000 B.C. Over a decade later, deeper layers of habitation were subjected to numerous tests and dated to 45,000 B.C. Niede Guidon, archaeologist and Director of Brazilian excavations, relates that this area of Brazil has over 400 prehistoric sites, including 340 cave paintings. In January 2000, Guidon also announced the results of carbon dating of a human

Costa Rica petroglyphs.
Source: *Handbook of South American Indians* (1948),
Bureau of Ethnology, U.S. Gov. Printing Office.

skull and three fossilized human jawbones. The bones were 15,000 years old. The response from American archaeologists was described by Guidon as "violent"—meaning that vicious verbal attacks were made on the research quality, her credibility, and South American archaeology in general. She added that "North American [archaeologists] criticize without knowledge."[4]

As previously mentioned, the Monte Verde site in southern Chile has now been dated from 33,000 to 37,000 years ago. In the central highlands of Peru, Pikimachay (Flea Cave), located in the Ayacucho Valley, has had several radiocarbon tests performed on layers of human habitation. These dates consistently fall in the 20,000-B.C. range. In addition, a rock shelter near Lagoa Santa in Brazil was dated to older than 23,000 B.C. It appears quite likely that some of the hundreds of other caves and rock shelters found throughout South America will eventually be dated from 20,000 to 50,000 years ago.

Numerous other early habitation sites have been found in South America dating to pre-Clovis. The Muaco site in Venezuela was dated to about 15,000 B.C. The nearby site of Taima-Taima was dated to 11,000 B.C. The El Abra rock shelter in Colombia dated to 10,400 B.C. In the Moche Valley of western Peru, several sites dated to older than 11,000 B.C. At Toca do Sitio do Mejo in Brazil several sites were dated between 10,400 B.C. and 12,300 B.C.

South America is covered with sites that have been dated to between 8,000 B.C. and 10,000 B.C. These include a huge shell mound on the mouth of the Tapajos River, where it flows into the Amazon; sites in the highlands of Ecuador; on Ecuador's arid Santa Elena Peninsula; the Talara tarseeps in extreme northwestern Peru; Ilo in southern Peru; Tagua-Tagua and associated sites in central Chile; the Rio Grande do Sol in southern Brazil; and numerous other locations. In Patagonia, a nearly arctic region in the extreme southernmost part of South America, several sites date to about 11,000 B.C.

South American archaeologists believe that a large and sophisticated maritime culture was fully developed on the shores of the

Petroglyphs in Argentina.
Source: *Handbook of South American Indians* (1949),
Bureau of Ethnology, U.S. Gov. Printing Office.

Pacific Ocean, certainly by 9000 B.C., but the ancestors of these people had already established themselves in the area much earlier. The western coast of South America has long been tectonically rising; thus many of the earliest sites are actually believed to be inland. In remote times extensive trading routes were established from the coast to the highlands, where large population centers existed.[3] Perhaps the best documented example of these ancient maritime civilizations was discovered on Ecuador's Pacific Coast. A September 8, 1998, article in *Science* revealed the existence of a 13,000-year-old coastal culture, termed "Las Vegas" because of its proximity to the Las Vegas River. Evidence showed that these people maintained an active maritime trade with coastal communities extending from Panama to Peru.

The Emerging Picture of South America's Remote Past

It should be apparent from the evidence acquired through the traditional methods of excavation, analysis, and dating techniques that ancient South America was extensively inhabited long ago. Strangely, the oldest sites appear to be in the Andes area, with reliable dating showing that there were certainly many different large "pockets" of people there by 50,000 B.C.— and probably in some central areas much earlier. There is only one date indicating occupation as early as 300,000 B.C., but then only one such test has been performed. Given the scornful response from their northern counterparts—and the fact that the major source of funding for excavations is from America—it's likely that some South Americans would hesitate to publish or publicize astounding results.

While we have an incomplete picture of South America's ancient past, there are a few more summary points that can be made. Areas along the Pacific Coast, especially along the middle two-thirds of the continent, appear to have been populated later than the Andes but still well before 10,000 B.C. An extensive maritime culture was already operating on the Pacific Coast before that time. Then, not long after 10,000 B.C., a major influx of people entered the continent eventually inhabiting all of it. However, it should be kept in mind that scientific archaeological research in South America is relatively recent, with the vast majority of excavations conducted after the 1980s. There were, however, an astonishingly large number of excavations and site reports gathered from early explorers and teams who trekked through the continent from the 1800s to the 1980s. These reports provide us with quite a bit of interesting information.

Mound Builders of the Amazon

In May 2002, *Discoverer* reported that a mound builder culture had been found in the heart of the Brazilian Amazon by an anthropologist from Chicago's Field Museum of Natural History. Long reported by pilots and a few adventurers, the mounds were more extensively explored from the 1980s to 2002. They were dated to about A.D. 200, and numerous manmade canals are also in the area. As reported in the prior section, however, a huge shell mound in the western Amazon (located in central Brazil) has been dated to about 8000 B.C.

Shell mounds over 70 feet high were common on the Pacific Coast of Brazil, but virtually all of them have been destroyed for construction materials. Some were carbon dated prior to their destruction and were in the 6000-B.C. range.[3]

In the 1940s and 1950s the Bureau of American Ethnology published a series of massive books detailing the tribes, cultures, and archaeological works in South America.[5] The volumes contain over 4000 pages and hundreds of photos of mounds, artifacts, cultural elements, and indigenous tribes. This series covers the extensive explorations and discoveries made in South America from the 1800s to the late 1940s.

Numerous shell and earthen mounds were discovered and excavated along the Paraná River Delta, beginning in 1877. The Paraná

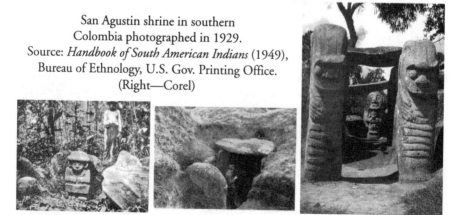

San Agustin shrine in southern
Colombia photographed in 1929.
Source: *Handbook of South American Indians* (1949),
Bureau of Ethnology, U.S. Gov. Printing Office.
(Right—Corel)

flows south from south central Brazil through Paraguay and Argentina, emptying into the Atlantic at Buenos Aires. The Delta begins in Paraguay, extending across Argentina. Along the river at Campana in Argentina, a large mound was excavated in 1877. "This monument was a tumulus similar to those found in the different territories of Europe and the Americas. ...Taking the form of an ellipse, its major diameter measures 220 feet; the lesser diameter was 90 feet; and its greatest height was 7 feet." Various pieces of pottery and human bones were recovered. The authors also described the existence of many similar mounds in the region. Within the same region is the Malabrigo River. Dozens of mounds containing artifacts and human remains were found on the riverbanks.

The best known mound culture of the Amazon was discovered in 1870 on Marajó Island, in the mouth of the Amazon, just below the equator. The "island" is only three feet above water, but it covers 14,000 square miles. Over 100 mounds were discovered in the 1800s on the island. The most famous of these was Pacoval first described in 1871. It was 290 feet long, 125 feet wide, and 13 feet high. An 1877 field survey found pottery "covering the ground like a great mosaic." In a single week a 1914 team recovered over 3,000 pieces.

The Anajás River also had numerous mounds. In 1885, the largest mound at that location was described as 680 feet long, 260 feet wide, and 42 feet high. Numerous huge, red-painted jars were recovered from the mound.[5]

None of the mounds reported in the 1800s have ever been dated, but it appears from the recent research that the mounds on the Atlantic Coast are far more recent than those found deeper into the Amazon or those on the Pacific Coast.

Small mounds and pit depressions at Tierra del Fuego.
Source: *Handbook of South American Indians* (1950), Bureau of Ethnology, U.S. Gov. Printing Office.

The Amazon mounds located in the western portion of the jungle (in mid-South America) definitely appear to be older than their Pacific counterparts. The huge, central-Brazilian mound at the Tapajos River dated to 8000 B.C., with the Pacific mounds falling in the 6000-B.C. range. Mounds located on the Atlantic Ocean side of the Amazon show fairly recent occupation—A.D. 200.

North American Mound Builders

By comparison, the North American mound builders began the practice as early as 3400-3000 B.C. in Louisiana, but 180 years later these people disappeared. Mound building in America resurfaced about 40 miles from the original Louisiana site *circa* 2000 B.C. From there, the practice moved up the Mississippi River into the Ohio River valleys, where it flourished, beginning 1500-1000 B.C. In brief, the mounds of South America are far older than any in America, and the entire continent appears to have been settled long before North America.

Typical skin covered hut in use in Amazon. Source: *Handbook of South American Indians* (1950), Bureau of Ethnology, U.S. Gov. Printing Office.

Below left: Early excavation of mound at Tierra del Fuego. Right: mound excavation. Source: *Handbook of South American Indians* (1950), Bureau of Ethnology, U.S. Gov. Printing Office.

Chapter 3

A Review Of Major South American Cultures — In Brief

Excavation and radiocarbon dating evidence from South American sites show that the continent was inhabited very early, certainly by 50,000 B.C.—and possibly as early as 300,000 B.C. For decades, the people who existed prior to 6000 B.C. or so have been referred to as "big game hunters," "paleo-Indian," "Clovis," "archaic," or "stone age." However, these terms are utilized because we really know little else about them. Evidence shows that they had sophisticated knowledge of the usage of herbal medicines, they traveled and traded extensively, and they also appear to have had a well-developed maritime technology—especially on the Pacific coast.

It is impractical to attempt a comprehensive review of all the hundreds of sites and cultural traditions of South America; therefore, only some of the most impressive and best known will be cited. The reader should note that the pictures in this book include many from the sites listed as well as from sites and artifacts in other parts of South America. This review especially centers on Peruvian locations, for a simple reason: more is known about these cultures than most other cultures in South America.

Ayacucho

The earliest "identifiable culture" in South America is considered by many to be the Ayacucho (Eye-ah-coo-choo), located in central Peru. The Ayacucho Basin has had at least 23 different civilizations, dating from 23,000 B.C. to A.D. 1470 and ranging from the Wari to the Inca.

Rather than a culture, Ayacucho is best described as a region where various cultures existed over a vast time period. Picimachey Cave (Flea Cave) is in the region and is located 24 kilometers north of Ayacucho City. Hundreds of bone and stone tools have been excavated at five different locations in the region, dating to as early as 23,000 B.C. Clay was used in some tools, hearths, and basins but not in the making of ceramics. Later groups at Ayacucho (*circa* 11,000 B.C.) hunted mastadon and other extinct game. Communal huts were commonly utilized as shelter. The huts were constructed from animal skins draped over sapling branches used as frames. In addition, "ceremonial" huts have been excavated containing medicinal plants and chewed leaves.[1, 2, 3]

Chilca Valley

The Chilca Valley lies between the puna zone, near the western coast of Peru, and the Pacific. The puna zone is a 12,000-foot-high area of open fields and sweeping winds. Archaeologists long believed the area to have been barren, but 1970s excavations in the area showed that

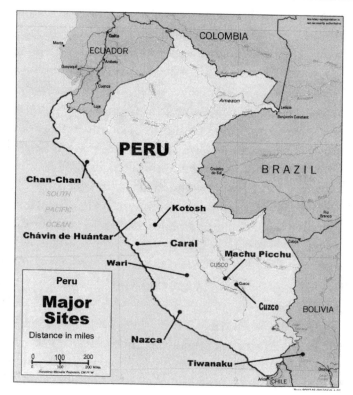

it had been important. Two sites, Tres Ventanas and Kiqche, dated 6000 B.C.– 2500 B.C., were located in the heart of Chilca Valley. The research at the sites showed that the valley was a frequently used trade route between the Pacific Coast and civilizations higher up in the Andes. Large trade networks centered in the valley where, several crops were grown.[4]

Caral & Associated Sites

The January 27, 2001, issue of *Science* announced the discovery of what has been since described as "America's Oldest City"—Caral— which is located about 120 miles north of Lima, Peru. Caral is one of 18 large, ancient complexes in the Supe Valley, a desert lying 14 miles from the Pacific. Archaeologists from both Peru and the United States excavated portions of the site, eventually carbon dating it to 2627 B.C. A puzzling mystery at Caral is that the culture was obviously advanced and sophisticated, yet no pottery or ceramics have ever been found.

Caral encompassed over 200 acres, centered on a huge plaza area ringed by six large, truncated (flat-topped) pyramids. Today the "pyramids" look like mounds, because centuries of looting and erosion badly deformed the baked-mud bricks used for their construction. The largest, the "Piramide Mayor," was 60 feet high, with a base 450 by 500 feet. The pyramids were built in one or two phases in a relatively brief time period. Thus a highly organized civilization must have been present there.

Caral also had three circular plazas, sunken below the ground surface level. The largest of these was 150 feet in diameter. A few archaeologists speculate that the Inca cultures probably evolved from the Caral civilization, because the Incas also utilized stone circles and had both elevated and sunken circular plazas. But most South American specialists discount this idea.

The Caral pyramids were covered with rooms, open areas, stairs, and other structures. Archaeologists believe that tunnels and rooms were probably present within the pyramids, but they have yet to investigate this possibility. Where the people of Caral came from is a mystery to archaeologists, especially when one considers the fact that Caral was completely established at a time when archaeologists believe that the pyramids of Egypt were only being started.

All but one of the other 17 "similar" complexes in the Supe Valley have not been excavated or dated, and most of them range in size

Caral
Archaeological site
reconstruction by
Dee Turman ©

from 40 to 60 acres. Pottery has never been found at any of them. However, probably all of them are believed to be related to Caral. One other important aspect of Caral and the other sites in the Supe Valley relates to agriculture. These ancient people successfully grew beans, squash, and cotton in arid, desert conditions. They are suspected of being the first large-scale civilization in the Americas to build extensive irrigation canals.

While Caral has been touted as the "first city" in the Americas, such a statement may be more hype than fact. It is the largest of the Supe Valley pyramid centers, but not the oldest. At Aspero, on the Supe River, a well-contained, 30-acre complex of seven large, truncated pyramids and six smaller ones was dated to 2700 B.C. The walls of the pyramids were constructed from quarried rock set in a mud mortar.[5]

Cupisnique, the Kotosh Tradition, & U-Shaped Pyramid Complexes

While cultures were flourishing everywhere in South America in 2000 B.C., a curious religious-based culture emerged in the highlands at Kotosh, near the headwaters of the Huallaga River. A square temple with rounded corners was found at the site, with a large stone hearth in the middle. Offerings burned in the hearth included crystals and feathers. The temple is called the Temple of the Crossed Hands, because of a unique clay panel found on the temple walls. The panel displays a pair of crossed human arms. The Kotosh Tradition spread over 150 miles to the north and south in 2000 B.C.

Not long after 2000 B.C., pottery and ceramics appear to have been made in South America. Although this dating is based on

Far left: Chavín feline motif pottery. Right: Pucara pottery from central Andes.
Source: *Handbook of South American Indians* (1949 & 1950), Bureau of Ethnology, U.S. Gov. Printing Office.

excavations and actual finds, it may be that some form of container were made prior to this time. In the lowlands a pottery style called Cupisnique has been found between the sites of Virú and Lambayeque. These sites were large ceremonial centers used with associated villages.

In the same era, on the central coast of Peru, a unique form of pyramid building was begun. In the Huara, Chancay, Chillón, Rímac, and Lurín Valleys, U-shaped, mud-brick pyramid complexes were erected. Many of these sites were built around 1750 B.C. and encompassed 50 acres. The main pyramid of these complexes averaged about 60 feet in height, with the two pyramid "arms" of the U-shape 10- 20-feet high. The pyramids were covered with elaborate plaster designs.[5]

Chavín

The Chavín culture is one of the best known in South America. It emerged about 1400 B.C., reaching its peak in 400 B.C. Chavín produced exquisite cloth, ceramics, musical instruments, art, and precious metal artifacts. The art forms of the Chavín are considered by most South American archaeologists to be similar to Olmec (the first culture recognized in Mexico). Chavín textiles and exquisite gold artifacts are some of the finest in the world.

The civilization reached its zenith at Chavín de Huántar, located in Peru 100 miles inland at nearly 10,000feet above sea level. Archaeologists speculate that 500 people may have lived near the massive temple complex that served as the focal point of the surrounding society. The site encompassed 37 acres spreading to both sides of the Wacheqsa River. A stone bridge, built about 500 B.C., spanned the river, connecting the two sides of the complex. The bridge was 10-feet wide and 23-feet long and was in use until a massive landslide destroyed it in 1945.

Early Venezuela pottery. Source: *Handbook of South American Indians* (1949), Bureau of Ethnology, U.S. Gov. Printing Office.

U-Shaped Complex
Archaeological site
reconstruction by
Dee Turman ©

Chavín de Huántar was situated to control trade routes between the coast and the highlands and was a major religious center. As an agricultural society, it had a large supporting population. The "Old Temple" was a U-shaped complex, opening to the east. The three temples comprising it were 36-, 52-, and 33-feet high, respectively. Drainage canals and numerous air ducts into the complex are believed to have served a purpose in the giving of oracles at the site. Tunnels, passageways, and numerous underground chambers (called galleries) have been found in many places in the complex as well as in the other temples associated with it. Many sculptures and obelisks have been found, with some depicting a jaguar's head with a shaman's body. Chavín pottery has a distinctive style and design motif copied by many other later groups.

As Chavín waned in 300 B.C., the cult spread to other locations. Some of these sites were initially discovered by looters, but it is known that many sites adopted the Chavín cultural tradition.[5, 6]

Moche Culture

The Moche lived along the northern Peruvian coastline and are considered to be a continuation of the earlier cultures that flourished in the area in 1500 B.C. Enormous irrigation networks had been well established before the Moche, but during their cultural development this practice was greatly expanded. Moche reached its peak between the years A.D. 1 and 700.

Sechín Alto—1500 B.C.

Sechín Alto was a massive site constructed in the Casma Valley in 1500 B.C. Left: focal point of the complex. Right: one of many "warrior" reliefs found at the site. Source: © Philip Baird/www.anthroarcheart.org.

Left: Chavín de Huántar—main portal to pyramid complex. Middle: examples of Chavín head carvings considered similar to Olmec. Bottom right: carving with serpent, condor, and feline characteristics. Third row left: Castillo de Chankillo, a Chavín ceremonial center.

Source: © Philip Baird/ www.anthroarcheart.org.

Left: Stone bridge at Chavín prior to its destruction. Source: *Handbook of South American Indians* (1949), Bureau of Ethnology, U.S. Gov. Printing Office.

Moche was a truly stratified society with an elite and ruling class that demanded sacrifices. Moche art and the designs found on their amazing pottery were long considered to be stylized representations of mythical, god-like figures, but recent excavations have proved that the brutal scenes of sacrifice and blood drinking shown on many ceramics represented real people and real events. Excavations in the tombs under Moche pyramids have uncovered the actual people represented in the painted scenes. Other Moche art depicts everything from acts of sex to illness to scenes from everyday life.

The Moche ruins of Sipán are not the largest, but have yielded fantastic treasure. Sipán lies in the middle of the La-Leche Valley, along the northern coast of Peru. In 1987 Dr. Walter Alva was called to the Moche ruins of Sipán because looters had partially uncovered a tomb inside one of the massive mud-brick pyramids at the site. A detailed excavation was subsequently performed, revealing the tomb and burial of the Mochia Sun-King, who was dubbed "The Lord of Sipán." He had been buried in A.D. 200 inside a wooden coffin tied together by three sets of copper straps. On both sides of the coffin a skeleton of a man and a sacrificed llama were found. They were surrounded by over 1100 decorated ceramic pots, with many depicting bound prisoners, blood sacrifices, and the drinking of blood by the King. Inside the coffin the King had been buried in full regalia with body-covering sheets of gilded gold and numerous other gold artifacts. The man inside the coffin

was dressed and adorned exactly as the regal person depicted on Mochia pottery who drank the blood of the sacrifices.

Other fantastic tombs at Sipán were soon excavated. These included the "Tomb of the Priest" and the "Tomb of the Old Lord of Sipán." Huge quantities of gold artifacts and ceramics were uncovered in these burials, including bizarre and otherworldly images. By 2002, 12 tombs had been excavated, dating from A.D. 100 to 300.[7]

The Sipán complex consists of three huge, mud-brick pyramids (called Huacas), with flat tops constructed in stages, beginning in about A.D. 100. The smallest is 33 feet tall with a base of 230 feet by 165 feet. All are badly eroded.

About 30 miles north of Sipán is Sicán, a later Moche site. Other Moche sites of great size and importance include the Huaca de la Luna and Huaca del Sol, Huancaco in Virú, Pampa de los Incas, Pañamarca, Mocollope, Galindo, and Pampa Grande. The later Moche sites, such

The Huaca del Sol. Source: © Philip Baird/www.anthroarcheart.org.

**Huaca del Sol
Archaeological site
reconstruction by
Dee Turman ©**

Sipán
Archaeological site
reconstruction by
Dee Turman ©

as Pampa Grande, contain extremely large pyramids. Huaca Fortaleza, the largest pyramid at Pampa Grande, was originally 125 feet tall with a base measuring 885 feet by 590 feet. A 950-foot-long ramp led to its summit. The top originally contained a complex of rooms, columns, and tunnels.[5]

Nazca

Nazca has been the source of some of the wildest speculation in any field of inquiry. The basis of this speculation has been the Nazca lines— gigantic images of insects, animals, and geometric forms drawn on the surface of the desert plain of Nazca.

By A.D. 100 the site of Cahuachi in the Nazca Valley was well established. The site continued to expand until 500. It served as a sacred site of pilgrimage, and numerous other Nazca culture complexes sprang up in the region. Nazca lies about 200 miles south of Lima on the barren, desert coastal plain. Cahuachi was probably established as the first settlement because the Nazca River emerges from

Examples of Mochia pottery. Source: *Handbook of South American Indians* (1949), Bureau of Ethnology, U.S. Gov. Printing Office.

underground at the site, providing a reliable source of water. Around A.D. 500, an extended drought caused the Nazca people to construct underground aqueducts and filtration systems.

The Nazca culture also constructed mud-brick pyramids, with the largest of these about 100 feet high. Lavish burial tombs have never been found in Nazca's pyramids, but the Nazca made beautifully designed pottery. The population estimates of the Nazca people have varied widely, but one Nazca complex, Pampa Grande, was home to at least 10,000 people. Another large population center was at Ventilla, which covered 495 acres.

Viewed from the ground the Nazca lines are not distinguishable as designs, but some of the surrounding mountains do give partial views of a few lines. They extend over 800 miles from the Nazca plains area into Chile, with the longest one 12 miles long. Two types of designs are found: desert floor drawings, made by removing the top layer of surface material; and hillside figures, made to be viewed from the ground. Space

aliens have been suggested as the builders of these enigmatic figures, but South American archaeologists have ventured what seems to be the most plausible speculation of exactly how the lines were drawn with such precision and accuracy. Some believe that hot-air balloons, constructed from animal skins or textiles, were employed as hovering sighting platforms. (A later chapter presents the research on this possibility.) The gigantic forms of whales, monkeys, birds, spiders, human forms, and other animals are depicted. In addition, various geometric designs are present. A variety of purposes have been proposed for them, including cylindrical devices; ceremonial site; sight lines; and "spirit paths," a pilgrimage road leading to sacred sites in the Andes. To date, no completely suitable answer has been confirmed. The Nazca culture largely disappeared around A.D. 750.[5, 6, 7]

Tiwanaku & Tihuanacao

About 1000 B.C. a religious-based culture developed in Bolivia, in the Titicaca basin near Lake Titicaca, a breathtaking 13,000 feet above sea level. The Tiwanaku culture spread over a wide area of influence but centered on the sites at Lake Titicaca. The sites of Chiripa and Pukara were the primary centers of this religion, and they lasted until A.D. 200. Pukara, north of the lake, covered nearly 1500 acres and had a U-

Above: the "spaceman" drawn on the Nazca Plain. Left: the Candelabra, the most famous of the lines designed to be seen from ground level. Seen from Pacific Ocean. Source: © Philip Baird/ www.anthroarcheart.org.

shaped set of temples and courtyards, stone buildings, and extensive residential areas. Chiripa extended over two square miles and had numerous pyramids with multiple levels, reaching its peak in A.D. 500. The pyramids and many walls at the site were constructed with large carved stone, perfectly fitted and matched to form nearly indestructible walls. The city is believed to have had 30,000-40,000 residents and was inhabited until A.D. 1000, when a protracted drought forced the population to leave. The Tiwanaku heartland of several cities and complexes also encompassed a large rural area and is believed to have been home to 365,000 people at its peak.

The focal point of Tiwanaku culture was on the south side of the lake in an area commonly called Tiahuanaco, which is located near a modern town with the same name. The name Tiahuanaco is not often utilized by South American archaeologists, who prefer to refer to the site and the culture as Tiwanaku. Tihuanacao, the center of the urban city near the south shore of the lake, was enclosed by a moat, which is believed to have been used to help irrigate the many raised agricultural terraces found there. The largest pyramid at Tihuanacao is called Akapana and was long believed to be a hilltop modified into a pyramid. Excavation of Akapana showed that it was constructed of precision-fitted quarried stone just as the other walls and pyramids at Tihuanaco. The upper walls appeared to have been deliberately destroyed when it was abandoned, giving it the appearance of a hill. A sunken court was erected atop the pyramid. Semi-subterranean temples are nearby, with massive platforms and gigantic monolithic statues. The famous Gateway of the

Below left: the entrance to Tiahuanaco's Kalasasaya Palace. Below right: The idol of Kalasasaya. Source: *Wonders of the Past* (1923).

Sun, a massive stone arch, cut from a single block of stone, is at the site. At some time in the remote past, it had been cracked by an earthquake. The figure depicted on the top central panel of the Gateway is widely regarded as Thunupa, a god-like being who was related to the sun and lightning.[4, 5, 6] (The legend of Thunupa is discussed in a later chapter.)

The people who inhabited Tiahuanaco are called the Aymara. They divided their territories into states and chiefdoms, with Tiahuanaco serving as the main capital. In truth, little is understood about these people who maintained a highly advanced civilization until their conquest by the Inca.

Top: Tiahuanaco's Gate of the Sun. Source:
Wonders of the Past (1923).
Below left: Tiahuanaco ruins. Right: idol from
Tiahuanaco. Source: *Corel.*

Chimú & Chan-Chan

About the time that the Tiwanaku empire was fading, on the coastal Pacific plains of Peru, the Chimú civilization arose from the remnants of the Moche and others. Chimú civilization began about A.D. 1000 and lasted to nearly 1500. The Chimú state became the largest on the coast, expanding through 800 miles of the coastal valleys. It is one of the best understood of all Peruvian cultures. The Chimú built huge and elaborate irrigation systems, with the longest irrigation canal extending 20 miles, from the Chicama River to Chan-Chan, the capital of the empire.

Chan-Chan was first established in 900, close to the Pacific Ocean, and it eventually reached a size of nearly eight square miles. Nine to 12 rectangular palace compounds, or citadels, were erected in the city, and all had imposing adobe walls, towering up to 30 feet in height. Sunken gardens, storerooms, platforms, and other structures literally cover the landscape of Chan-Chan. It is believed that the earlier

The massive size of Chan-Chan is evident in this 1930s aerial photo.
Source: *Handbook of South American Indians* (1949),
Bureau of Ethnology, U.S. Gov. Printing Office.

Wari civilization was the inspiration for the huge walls fortifying the city.

Five huge adobe pyramids once towered over the city, with the largest believed to have been 70 feet in height. But all of them have been almost completely destroyed by looters. A 1604 legend related that Chan-Chan was established by a man called Tacaynamu, who came from the north on a balsa raft. He sent each of his three sons to the north, south, and east, respectively, where they subdued and ruled the people already in the lands.

The people of Chan-Chan lived in small, irregularly-shaped adobe rooms, erected among the huge palace compounds. Local

Above: view of the extensive walls and remains from Chan-Chan. Bottom: view of plastered designs on walls at the Huaca del Dragon near Chan-Chan. Source: © Philip Baird/www.anthroarcheart.org.

neighborhoods formed around the palaces with narrow winding streets and passageways. Textiles, gold, silver, bronze artifacts, and ceramics were produced. At least 20,000 people lived in the city.

The Chimú empire expanded in A.D. 1150, eventually establishing major cities and compounds at Farfán, Reque, La Leche, and Túcume. The massive city of Pacatnamú, with 37 adobe brick pyramids, was also probably a Chimú center.

The demise of the Chimú culture and Chan-Chan is believed to have been caused by its expansive tendencies. The final ruler of Chan-Chan was Minchançaman. While attempting to conquer areas farther south, his forces encountered the Inca in 1462. Chan-Chan was conquered by the Incas about 1475, and Minchançaman was taken to Cuzco as a hostage. The people of Chan-Chan left the city quickly, abandoning unfinished pots and other artifacts.[1, 4, 5, 6]

Above: fish motif on wall plaster frieze at Tshudi complex at Chan-Chan. Right: details of one of the palace complexes at Chan-Chan. Bottom: view of the Chimu complex near Chan-Chan. Source: © Philip Baird/www.anthroarcheart.org.

Inca (Inka), Cuzco, Sacsawaman, & Machu Picchu

The Inca empire ultimately extended down the Pacific coastline, taking in nearly two-thirds of all the South American coast, including parts of Ecuador, Peru, Bolivia, Chile, and Argentina. Between 1200 and 1535 A.D., the Incas connected their expansive lands with an astonishing 15,500 -mile-road network. The Spanish took full advantage of the roads during the conquest. In 1555, Pedro de Ciezade León gave this description of the roads: "through deep valleys and over mountains, through piles of snow…along turbulent rivers…smooth and paved, carefully laid out…cut through rock with walls skirting the rivers, and steps and rests…everywhere…clean swept and kept free of rubbish, with lodgings, storehouses…temples…and posts."

The Incas had an organized, fierce, and powerful army conquering all opposition until the Spanish arrived with guns and an

Views of the ruins at Cuzco. Source: *Corel.*

insatiable lust for gold. The Inca military organization is reminiscent of the Roman Legions. Inca conquest began with the takeover of the Moche region. As their population and area of influence expanded, they built fortresses high in the Andes to protect the rulers and elite classes. Irrigation systems and terraced agriculture methods were widely employed in the growing of what are today thought of as modern crops: tomatoes, potatoes, yams, peanuts, and cotton. Taxes were collected from all residents and used to maintain the army, the ruling classes, religious and political structures, and the road system.

None of the Inca cities were as large as Chan-Chan, but their construction and quality is unsurpassed. The capital and most famous city was Cuzco, located in the eastern Peruvian Andes at 11,000 feet above sea level, overlooking a tributary of the Urubamba River. It was home to between 40,000 and 100,000 people. It was a carefully planned, multi-leveled city, perhaps laid out to represent a puma. From the Temple of the Sun in the center of Cuzco, over 40 sight lines radiated out, allowing an unrestricted view. The city was divided into four main sections, based on the four major "royal roads" that exited Cuzco to other parts of the empire. Plazas, palace and temple compounds, and other structures at the core of the city were built from quarried stone. Residential areas were constructed from adobe and stone, had wooden ceiling beams, and were covered with grass roofs.

Overlooking the city of Cuzco was Sacsawaman, an impenetrable fortress-looking complex constructed from gigantic limestone blocks

View of the ruins at Cuzco. Source: *Corel.*

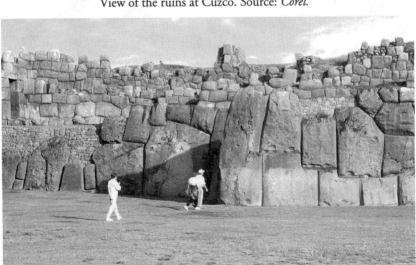

weighing nearly 100 tons each. Each stone was quarried and polished to exactly fit with the adjacent stones. No mortar was used nor was it necessary. Two huge towers were constructed above the walls. While Sacsawaman is usually described as a fortress, it is far more likely that it was home to priests or was used as a ceremonial site.

The Urubamba River Valley was covered with agricultural terraces, and beautifully constructed, carefully laid out towns are found almost everywhere across the landscape. Most of the town structures were built with stone, and many still look usable today. A network of tributary roads connected all the towns to Cuzco—no matter how remote they were.

While Cuzco served as the capital of the vast Inca Empire, it was necessary to build and maintain a provincial capital system. Huánuco Pampa, 435 miles north of Cuzco, was one of the most impressive. Huánuco Pampa covered 495 acres, had 4000 buildings, and 30,000 in

Right: the Stone of 12 Angles at Cuzco. Source: *Wonders of the Past* (1923)

Bottom: view of Inca stone on right side—modern wall on left. Source: © Philip Baird/ www.anthroarcheart.org.

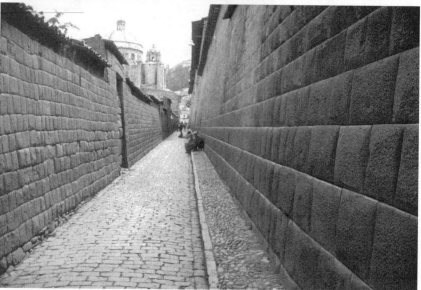

population in the city and adjacent area. The city center was a huge stone platform surrounded by fitted-stone temples, buildings, stairways, and palaces. There were so many Inca towns and cities, most of which remain in good preservation, that a visitor could spend years trying to visit each of them.

For a number of reasons, the site of Machu Picchu seems to hold the most mystery and fascination for North Americans. It was situated to be completely hidden from view until one actually arrived there, and was located in an extremely remote, nearly inaccessible area. It lies about 40 miles northwest of Cuzco and is archaeologically considered to be a "small" Inca town, perhaps serving as a retreat for

Right: the ruins of the Inca city of Intihuatana. Source: *Wonders of the Past* (1923)

Bottom right: view of ingenious vertical irrigated terraces. Left: colossal stone portal at Ollantaytambo. Source: © Philip Baird/ www.anthroarcheart.org.

priests or the elite. Its discovery in 1911 created a great deal of publicity, and many considered it to be the last Inca citadel.

Most of Machu Picchu's foundations were carved from the stone on the mountaintop it occupies. Temples, plazas, residential buildings, and support structures cover the site, along with the terraced slopes used for cultivation.

The Spanish conquest of the Inca was rapid. Pizarro captured the *Inca Sapa* (the King) in 1532, and by 1535 the conquest of the Inca Empire was complete.[1, 2, 5]

Who Were The Inca?

Archaeologists from both North and South America make a clear distinction and utilize a specific description when stating exactly who the Inca were. As the Inca Empire expanded, it took in the populations of the areas that were absorbed. However the added populations were not Inca, they were 'subjects' of the Empire. At its height, the Inca Empire had over 10 million subjects. Therefore, "the term 'Inca' refers

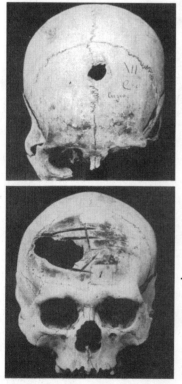

only to a small group of kindred, less than 40,000 individuals, who built a great Andean state by force…and who ruled as the realm's governing nobility."[2] The Inca "was a closed ethnic body" whose origins are steeped in mythology. (See the later chapter on South American Myth.) Their founders came to Cuzco as a small group of brothers and sisters and were more advanced than the indigenous peoples. Over many generations, their numbers increased, but they were careful to maintain an ethnic separation from outside people.

Right: the Inca and earlier people at Cuzco practiced trephination, a form of skull surgery that was often survived. Sometimes gold was placed over the openings. Source: *Handbook of South American Indians* (1949), Bureau of Ethnology, U.S. Gov. Printing Office.

Views of Machu Picchu. Source: *Corel.*

View of Machu Picchu's famous "hitching stone." Source: *Corel.*

Views of Inca stonework.
Source: © Philip Baird/www.anthroarcheart.org.

Chapter 4

Recent Genetic Contributions to South American Archaeology: Proof of Cayce's Atlantis and Mu?

Genetic research can be extremely difficult to understand. Compounding the problem is the fact that there are several different types of genetic research being conducted to try to identify our earliest ancestors. The purposes of this genetic research are to identify the exact place of origin of humanity, to precisely date when the first humans appeared, and to exactly determine when these ancient peoples migrated to various parts of the world. Making it even more difficult to understand is the speculation that accompanies this research and the arguments for competing theories. It can be overwhelmingly confusing. It's nearly impossible for a non-specialist to fully understand the complexities of how this research is conducted, and it seems inexplicable to most people how geneticists can assess when a particular group left a particular area.

Actually, relatively few studies have utilized human DNA in this process. A brief explanation of why this is the case is necessary, because it leads to the type of genetic research that dominates the hunt for ancient migration patterns. The original intention of genetic research is a noteworthy point meriting mention. All the ancient DNA research began as an effort to identify diseases and other characteristics in DNA. No one really suspected that a DNA trail would be found to the ancient past, and its discovery took nearly everyone by surprise.

Human DNA (nDNA)

Human DNA lies in the nucleus of virtually every cell in the human body. It consists of roughly three billion pairs of four different amino acids. The three billion pairs of amino acids (called base pairs) are linked together, forming the steps or rungs of what can be thought of as a long ladder.

Imagine that you were constructing a ladder with three billion steps. But each step of the ladder, rather than being a single piece, had to be made by snapping together two smaller pieces and then attaching the ends of the pieces to the sides of the ladder. There are four possible choices for each of the two pieces of each step, and there are some rules about how the pieces must be fit together. That, in essence, is the human genetic code.

Now, rather than being rigid, like a ladder is supposed to be, imagine that it was made from strips of rubber bands and is flexible. After the ladder is completed, it is then twisted together tightly. If you take a piece of a rubber band and twirl its two ends in different directions, what eventually results is a tightly wound ball. In fact, the human DNA that resides in the nucleus of the cells looks a lot like a tightly wound ball.

The actual physical size of a cell, its nucleus, and the tightly wound DNA within it is mind-boggling. The average diameter of a human brain cell is 1/10,000 of an inch. The nucleus is much smaller, and the DNA within the nucleus is smaller still. Now for the part that defies the comprehension of just about everyone, including those who work in the field of genetics.

Imagine we could remove a single ball of the wound DNA from a single cell. Then imagine we could unwind it and lay it flat without stretching or breaking it. If you could see it (which you couldn't with the naked eye), it would look a lot like a long ladder. More specifically—

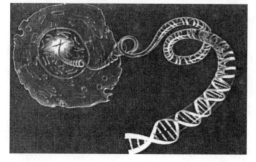

Strand of human DNA depicted as unwinding from the nucleus. Source: *Psychopharmacology* (1997), NIDA illus.

a really, really, long ladder. The strand of DNA in your cells would be an astonishing six feet long. The average human body has somewhere in the vast neighborhood of 50 trillion cells, and virtually all of them except blood cells have a six-foot-long strand of DNA in them.[1]

Obviously, research that attempted to compare the three billion pairs of amino acids making up the "steps of the ladder" from one person to another would be unbelievably difficult—not to mention excessively expensive. Luckily, there are certain portions of the ladder's steps that are more important than others, and those are the portions that the human DNA studies have assessed. But one other difficulty arises in this line of research. The human DNA strand is fragile, and over time, it degrades. Thus the testing of ancient remains depends on obtaining preserved samples of DNA, and that has proved to be a difficult task.

Mitochondrial DNA Analysis: Understanding the Mitochondria

An understanding of the most frequently employed DNA research attempting to trace the origins of humanity requires a brief explanation of the specific kind of DNA that is used. This DNA is *not* human DNA. *But it is found everywhere in the human cells.* Understanding it is made easier by explaining its purpose and the disease diabetes.

Most people know that diabetes is related to the hormone insulin and blood sugar. Insulin is critical in the movement of glucose molecules (sugar) into the cells of the body, where they are utilized as "fuel." People commonly believe that the cells of the body somehow "burn" sugar for energy, but that is not exactly accurate. More on that issue in a moment, but for now, let's return to insulin.

When insulin is released into the bloodstream by the pancreas, the molecules of the hormone move into small "holes" on the walls of cells that are shaped in such a manner as to make the insulin tightly fit into them. These small holes are known as receptor sites. When a receptor site is filled by an insulin molecule, it opens up channels, or passages, in the cell wall, and a small protein moves from the inside of the cell to the outside of the cell. After reaching the outside of the cell, this transporter protein grabs a molecule of glucose and pulls it back inside the cell.

The molecule of glucose is delivered to a small organelle (described momentarily) located within the cell called a mitochondrion.

A single mitochondrion is shaped a bit like a football, but it has to be kept in mind that the physical size of all this area of activity is small—so small as to be nearly incomprehensible.

The mitochondrion essentially "ingests" the molecule of glucose, and in a whirlwind of activity on its body, it pulls in free-floating protons and phosphorous. As a result of this complicated process, what eventually emerges from the other end of the mitochondrion is a molecule of ATP—adenosine triphosphate. The ATP is the energy that keeps us alive and maintains all the activity in the cells.[2]

When diabetes is present, the transport of glucose into the cells is hampered, because there is either no insulin being produced by the pancreas or too little insulin.

What Are The Mitochondria?

Human cells actually contain hundreds to many thousands of these little energy-producers. (The plural of mitochondrion is *mitochondria*.) The mitochondria are believed to be specialized bacteria that allowed evolution from simple, single-celled life to complex life forms, composed of trillions of cells working together. They multiply as needed on their own for a simple reason—they carry their own DNA just as all other bacteria do.

In contrast to the three billion pairs of amino acids in human DNA, the mitochondria have only 16,569. The mitochondrial sequence was completely worked out and published in 1981. In addition, rather than being tightly wound like human DNA, mitochondrial DNA is arranged into a circular pattern. These factors make research on mitochondrial DNA (abbreviated as mtDNA) far easier.

Simplifying mtDNA research even more was a discovery that reduced the number of base pairs needed for analysis. Only about one thousand base pairs have to be assessed to obtain the needed information. Finally, mtDNA does

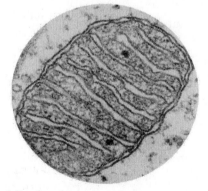

Mitochondrion magnified by electron microscope. Source: *Psychopharmacology* (1997), NIDA illus.

not degrade as easily or as quickly as does human DNA. Under ideal conditions, mtDNA from well-preserved samples as old as 100,000 years can sometimes be analyzed. Tooth and bone samples are typically utilized for analysis of ancient human remains.

Because they are not based on human DNA, the mitochondria that enter a developing fetus all come from the unborn infant's mother. Thus the mitochondria in all people, men and women, are inherited from the mother, who, in turn, received her mitochondria from her mother, and so on—all the way back to the very first female human being. This individual is known as "Mitochondrial Eve." The earliest accepted date of Mitochondrial Eve's existence is 200,000 B.C. But this date is based on an assumption seldom mentioned in the literature. It is not just possible, but it's already been found that some types of mtDNA have been extinct. These extinct forms of mtDNA may eventually point to other Mitochondrial Eves, who lived far earlier than 200,000 B.C. and in other locations on earth.

Mitochondrial Mutation — A Time Machine

For a host of reasons, some of which are known, all DNA, whether human or mitochondrial, mutates. This means that small changes can occur in the base pairs of the code over time. The rate of mtDNA mutation is much faster than mutation in human DNA— about ten times faster. Thus, when a mother passes on her mutated mtDNA to her offspring, they retain the mutated form. As her female offspring have their children, they are given the specific mutated form of the mtDNA and so on, through subesquent generations as the lineage progresses. The first female to have a particular mtDNA mutation is a sort of "miniEve," who is the first of a subsequent lineage passed on to her offspring.

Because the rate of mtDNA mutation is known, it can be reliably predicted (within certain ranges of certainty) exactly when a particular mutation occurred. In addition, within a particular type of mutation, more mutations can occur. But again, the date of that mutation can be reliably predicted. Geneticists are thus able to go back in time with each mutational strain and know, within limits, when it developed. MtDNA analysis is therefore a sort of time machine that enables us to look back through time to the first ancestors of a particular lineage.

Human beings have always been mobile and expansive, moving to different areas of the world. When the offspring of these migrating peoples multiplied so much as to create a large population in a particular area, some of them migrated to other areas. Thus mtDNA research throughout the world shows that different regions tend to have clusters of particular mutational types centered in them. Such clusters are actually groups of related types of mtDNA.

Current research shows that mtDNA has developed into 42 major groupings called **haplogroups.** (Note that more haplogroups will eventually be identified.) There are some sub-groupings within these, and the term *haplotypes* has been employed to describe them.

The first studies utilizing this type of testing were performed on Native Americans, and the first four types identified, for the sake of convenience, came to be called by letters: A, B, C, and D. As more haplogroups were identified, researchers continued to apply letters to them and add subgroup numbers as needed. A brief and incomplete summary of the major haplogroups is as follows: The L (L1, L2, and L3) group is considered a southern African lineage. Nine groups (H, I, J, K, T, U, V, W, and X) contain the vast majority of mtDNAs from European, North African, and Western Asia Caucasians. Haplogroups A, B, C, D, E, F, G, and M embrace the majority of the lineages found in Asia, Oceania, and Native Americans.

Haplogroup Origins

For complex reasons, some based on logic and reasonable speculation, Mitochondrial Eve is believed to have lived in Africa 200,000 years ago. The research and reasoning behind this assumption is based on a host of scientific studies conducted on the mtDNA of people living around the world.

As mentioned earlier, the many major divisions of the world tend to have high levels of only a few haplogroups within each region. These specific haplogroups can then be traced to earlier forms of the haplogroup (via the mutational time machine) and then matched to people living in other areas of the world. For example, in the case of the first research on Native Americans, haplogroups A, B, C, and D were identified. When A, C, and D were later discovered in people living in Siberian Asia, this led the researchers to reasonably assume that A, C, and D came to America from Asia. Small variations (meaning small mutations) could be identified in the American versions of A, C, and D, leading the researchers to see that the American forms of the haplogroups were more recent.

It would be inaccurate to state that *all* researchers believe in the following assessment, but the world's mtDNA types tend to coalesce in—or point to—Africa. However, it is important to understand that scientists can only point to areas of the world that still exist as a site of origin. For example, a specific haplogroup termed "X" has no known origin. But because the "Out of Africa" theory holds sway over current thinking, it is assumed that it came from Africa and spread to Asia. If haplogroup X originated in a land that is no longer in existence, the research couldn't possibly show it.

North American Genetics & Truly Ancient DNA

In attempts to trace the origins of Native North Americans, numerous studies were conducted on the mtDNA of living members of various tribes, beginning in the late 1980s. By early 1997, geneticists were convinced that the research had proven that the Native Americans had all come from Siberia, just as archaeologists had long-asserted. (Haplogroups A, B, C, and D were found, and all were believed to have originated in Asia. Haplogroup B was mainly restricted to China and Japan.)

But the estimates of the time of migration (based on the rate of mutation) didn't match the 9500 B.C.-migration date that archaeologists had insisted was correct. Instead, the research showed that the first people from Siberia entered well before 30,000 B.C. In addition, the data also showed that several other migrations had probably occurred: in 28,000 B.C. and 10,000 B.C.

In 1997 the Clovis-first idea collapsed with the Monte Verde announcement. And with the deeper layers at Monte Verde showing that it had been occupied as early as 37,000 years ago, confirmation of the genetic data was made. This made it obvious to some researchers that the genetics could be combined with archaeological work to really make the events in the ancient world clearer.

Later in 1997, geneticists found the presence of haplogroup X in some Native Americans—exclusively in the Southwest and the Northeast—in the traditional Iroquois lands. Because haplogroup X was not known to be in Asia, it was immediately branded as an obvious post-historical intrusion into Native American groups. That means that they assumed that it *must* have entered with European settlers who had mixed with the native tribes. That reasoning satisfied the archaeological community, who were still certain that all Native Americans came from Siberia.

Not long after, studies were published that had performed mtDNA analysis on the remains of individuals who had been buried in mounds in north central America. Sometime thereafter many studies reported on the testing of ancient remains recovered from burials from other parts of the United States. As with the living Native Americans, haplogroup X showed up — in about 4 percent of the remains. But in the Northeast, in the traditional lands of the Iroquois, it was in nearly 25 percent of some tribes as well as in ancient remains. Then haplogroup X was found in several individuals who had died over 8000 years ago in Florida. All these remains were so old that the implications were crystal clear: haplogroup X had to have entered America thousands of years before historical times.

The time estimates on haplogroup X entering America were at first shaky, because too few samples had been taken. But later, it seemed that haplogroup X entered by 28,000 B.C. and again in 10,000 B.C.

Haplogroup X in Europe, the Middle East, & the Gobi: Confirming Cayce's Atlantis Migrations

In a 2001 study haplogroup X was identified in ancient remains (6000-8000 years old) found in several cemeteries in the traditional area occupied by the Basque—the Pyrenees Mountains of France and Spain. Haplogroup X was also found in Egypt and Israel in relatively high numbers. In 2001 it was also found in a small tribe living in the

Altaic Mountain region of the Gobi Desert. This excited the archaeological community, because they considered it "proof" that all the Native Americans had come from Asia. But it is important to note that geneticists do not consider haplogroup X to have come from Asia—they simply don't know its origin.

Small numbers of people in Finland and Italy have also been found with haplogroup X, and it is notable that a few Cayce readings make mention of these areas—linking them to Atlantis.

While Edgar Cayce's story of the ancient Americas hasn't been fully presented yet, it is necessary to make mention of a few facts. A subsequent chapter will more fully review his readings on migrations from Atlantis and Mu, but a brief review will be helpful. Cayce stated that groups of Atlanteans migrated from their island several times and to several locations. The dates he gave for these migrations center on the years 28,000 B.C. and 10,000 B.C. Interestingly, these are the same dates geneticists believe migrations were made to the Americas. Cayce also gave the destinations of the major Atlantean migrations—to the Iroquois lands, America's Southwest, the Pyrenees Mountains, the Middle East, and the Gobi area—the exact places where haplogroup X has been found. Cayce also told of migrations to Central and South America, and momentarily, we'll review what has been found in these areas. But the implication was clear to us. Haplogroup X may well be the Atlantean version of mtDNA. Our earlier book, *Mound Builders,* presents much of the research leading to this idea.

America's Clovis & Europe's Solutrean Culture: Survivors of Cayce's Atlantis?

The fact that Clovis-like artifacts or Clovis cultural remnants have never been found in Siberia should be a genuine sticking point in archaeological theory, but it has never been so. Clovis has been described as a thundering horde of "big-game hunters" who came down from Siberia in 10,000 B.C., quickly exterminating all the huge, dangerous herds of animals that roamed the Americas. They seem to have acquired their "advanced big-game hunting technology" the moment they arrived, since they don't appear to have carried it with them. The current ideas still assert, and rightly so, that a large group of advanced people (advanced for the 10,000-B.C. time frame) did enter America in 10,000 B.C. They seem to have gone everywhere in the Americas quickly, not only exterminating the large animals, but also some groups of people already living in the Americas.

It has long been known that a European culture known as Solutrean came into the Spain, France, and Portugal areas a few thousand years before Clovis. Interestingly, America's Clovis is essentially identical to Europe's Solutrean. The separation in time between the two cultures (several thousand years) has kept American archaeologists from theorizing that they had the same source, but the Cayce readings certainly explain it.

According to Cayce, Atlantis was located close to the Caribbean Ocean, and by 10,000 B.C. Atlanteans were the world's "Red Race." We are aware that some writers—even those of Edgar Cayce-oriented books—have characterized Atlanteans as "white," but Cayce never did so. Ne clearly stated that Atlanteans were the Red Race. Most of these writers base their statements on a host of questionable books written in the 1800s and early 1900s, which are based on the blatantly biased idea of "whites" as the most advanced race. Cayce is thrown into the writing in a manner that leads the reader to believe Cayce referred to Atlanteans as white.

In the Cayce readings it is related that several migrations from Atlantis went to the Pyrenees area well before the last remaining islands were destroyed in 10,000 B.C. If these people carried the Clovis-like culture with them, then that explains why the Solutrean Culture preceded America's Clovis.

In truth, after Clovis collapsed and the genetic evidence on haplogroup X was released in 1997, a few archaeologists did speculate on the connection between Clovis and Solutrean. This speculation came after haplogroup X was found in a small Finnish population. *The Solutrean Culture, they reasoned, must have come to America over an ice bridge that connected Scandinavia to Iceland to Greenland to North America.* These people must have brought the cultural traits with them that became known as America's Clovis.

Less than a decade ago, an academic who expressed that idea would have been shunned and professionally destroyed. Such a journey was considered completely impossible. But with the emerging data, archaeologists are scrambling to somehow explain findings that were considered to be "impossible" only a few years ago.

The Atlantis explanation countering the Europe-America ice-bridge theory is simple and elegant and explains the archaeological facts and the genetic data far better. Between 28,000 B.C. and 10,000 B.C., groups of people bearing the X haplogroup migrated from a central location between America and Europe. They first migrated to Europe, carrying with them a culture that came to be known as Solutrean. As it became obvious that their land was soon going to be completely destroyed, in 10,000 B.C. groups of people bearing the X haplogroup migrated from this central location to several places in the Americas. They carried the same cultural traits to America, where the artifact types came to be called Clovis. Plato called this central location Atlantis—as did Edgar Cayce. All the places in the world where haplogroup X is found are places where Cayce stated the Atlanteans went, and the dates of the migrations match Cayce's. If the correlation between the information given in the Cayce readings and the current evidence is a coincidence, it falls far out of the range of statistical probability that science accepts as due to chance.

Advanced Technology In Atlantis

By utilizing a simplistic line of reasoning, several archaeological textbooks and a few archaeologists appearing in documentaries have tried to show that all Atlantis speculations are ridiculous. They vaguely refer to Cayce readings that state the Atlanteans had advanced technology—flying ships, lasers, and other kinds of gadgets. Why, they ask, aren't such devices found here? If Atlanteans were so advanced, why didn't they bring these things with them when they came in 10,000 B.C.? Then they answer their own question—because Atlantis never existed.

The answer to this reasoning is found in the Cayce readings. In 28,000 B.C. the technology of Atlantis was completely destroyed, when a violent series of events broke it up into islands. In our 2002 documentary, *Mound Builders: Edgar Cayce's Forgotten Legacy*, Edgar Evans Cayce, Cayce's son and the author of two best-selling books on

Cayce's Atlantis readings, stated that his research had confirmed this idea. The peak of Atlantis technology was before 28,000 B.C., and the majority of the population was killed during the catastrophic events. Their raw materials, factories, and technology suddenly disappeared, sending the few remaining survivors back to the Stone Age.

By 10,000 B.C. they had become the most advanced culture in existence again, far more advanced than any other group. But their technology was lithic—based on stone tools, because that's all the survivors had to work with in starting over from scratch. A sort of one-person example of how this probably worked was in the movie *Cast Away* in which Tom Hanks plays the part of a Federal Express executive who became stranded on a remote island. After a month or so on the island, he was living a stone-age-era life, despite the fact that he had the knowledge of modern technology.

South American Genetics

A host of genetic studies have emerged from various places in South America. Most of these have focused on living South Americans, but more are now being published on the analysis of remains. The studies have painted a sometimes-confusing picture to traditional theorists, but fall in perfect line with Cayce's ideas.

Haplogroups A, B, C, and D have been found in ancient remains tested throughout all of South America, all the way down to the southern tip of the continent. This indicated to geneticists that the inhabitants of North and South America were, indeed, related. But that statement gives an incomplete understanding of what is now known. For example, the Yanomami tribe, living in the Amazon, is primarily haplogroup A, B, C, and D, but three other as-yet-unidentified haplogroups were inexplicably found. How many new haplogroups will eventually be identified in South America is anybody's guess, but every new study shows more of them. The general interpretation of "unknown haplogroups" is straightforward. Unless they are eventually found in living populations, they are now extinct. All the members of that lineage simply died off or were intentionally killed.

Ancient Moche DNA

An extremely important study was presented and published in the *Proceedings of the Biomolecular Conference* (April 2002).[3] An international team of investigators performed mtDNA analysis on remains (a tooth sample from each person) recovered from tombs of the mud-brick pyramids at Sicán, Sipán, and the Huaca de la Luna—all from Moche Culture tombs dating from about A.D. 900. Chapter Three included some photos and a description of two of these sites, including the fantastic excavation of The Lord of Sipán.

At Sicán, 29 individuals' remains, including 22 females believed to be from the elite classes, were tested. They were removed from two separate tombs where some sort of orderly and intentionally grouped burials had been made.

From Sipán, 16 individuals' remains were recovered, but sufficient samples from teeth allowed only 10 of them to be tested. The Lord of Sipán, The Old Lord of Sipán, the Priest, and a young woman who was buried next to him in the Priest's Tomb were successfully tested.

At the Huaca de la Luna, the remains from 70 young males who had been sacrificed were removed, and 16 were subsequently tested. They had been decapitated, dismembered, and mutilated *circa* A.D. 500.

Results of the mtDNA tests were intriguing. The Lord of Sipán, The Old Lord of Sipán, and the young woman buried with the Priest were maternally related. The Priest was maternally related to two of the four females buried with him. The mtDNA haplogroups at Sipán included A (11 percent), B (33 percent), C (11 percent), and D (33 percent). Interestingly, the remainder of the individuals fell into three mtDNA types classified as "Other." The three imperial burials were all haplogroup A.

At Sicán, 12 of the 22 females were maternally related, and they were grouped on the north and south sides of the tomb. Of the 29 Sicán remains tested, 18 percent were haplogroup A, 25 percent were haplogroup B, 0 percent were C, and about 4 percent were D. Over half (57 percent) were classified into unique and unknown haplogroups ("Other").

Surprisingly, all of the sacrificial victims at Huaca de la Luna, as well as the few individuals who had been carefully buried in the same location, shared the same haplogroup. All of them were haplogroup A.

It is interesting that the family of The Lord of Sipán was haplogroup A and that the victims sacrificed at Huaca de la Luna, some 100 miles in distance, were all haplogroup A. The authors suggest some sort of intra-group warfare may have been the cause.

The use of "Other" to describe the handful of unknown haplogroups discovered in the samples was intriguing, so a coauthor of the article presenting the above results, Dr. Izumi Shimada, Professor of Anthropology at Southern Illinois University, was contacted for comments in this book. He wrote, "Nobody can specify what the 'other' haplogroups were — at least yet. Although the four defined haplogroups (A-D) seem to effectively account for the present-day indigenous populations, there are a variety of reasons to think there were other haplogroups in ancient times."

mtDNA Studies From Peru & Brazil

Several studies have obtained mtDNA samples from both living Peruvians residing in the Andes as well as on ancient remains recovered there. It must be recalled that haplogroup X was not defined as such until 1997. Prior to that time, it was classified as "other"—just as in the Moche study described above. Pre-1997 studies on ancient remains in Peru, Ecuador, Panama, and Costa Rica identified "other" in about 3-5 percent of mtDNA samples. A, B, C, and D haplogroups were identified in all of these countries.

Several recent studies have discovered haplogroup X in both ancient remains as well as in small numbers of South American populations. In central Brazil, for example, haplogroup X turned up in remains found in 4000-year-old burial pots. And a 2000 study published in the *American Journal of Human Genetics*[4] found that 3 percent of southern Brazilians are haplogroup X. In addition, haplogroup X is present in parts of Mexico, where little testing has thus far been done. The populations in Central and South America showing haplogroup X are low, somewhere between 1 and 3 percent—just as with Native North Americans.[5]

Musings on Haplogroup X
— The Newest Evidence

Haplogroup X may—or may not—turn out to be Atlantean mtDNA, but quite recent evidence provides even more support for Cayce's story of Atlantean migrations. As stated earlier, Cayce placed the Atlantean migrations to North America in two waves: the first, *circa* 28,000 B.C.; the second in 10,000 B.C.

In addition, Cayce indicated that a group of Atlanteans went to the Yucatan in 10,000 B.C. on a special mission. They were to establish a Hall of Records identical to the one in Egypt. (See *The Lost Hall of Records* for full details.) This group is believed to have gone to Piedras Negras, Guatemala. After burying the records in a temple, they remained in Yucatan establishing families. According to Cayce, at a time well after 3000 B.C., the descendants of these Atlanteans migrated north into America with another group. They eventually moved up the Mississippi River and into the Ohio River Valley, settling in the Ohio and northeast area, where the Mound Builder culture flourished. This final migration took place at least a thousand years after 3000 B.C., and in our book *Mound Builders* we showed that their arrival in Ohio was no earlier than 1500 B.C. When these descendants of the Yucatan Atlanteans reached the Ohio Valley area, they joined with the descendants of the Atlanteans who had gone to the Iroquois lands in 10,000 B.C.

While there is some strong evidence in traditional archaeology for this quite specific—and fairly complex—scenario, we never dreamed that genetic research could confirm any of it. But in 2002, strong confirmation of the 1500-B.C. Ohio migration emerged from genetics.

In an effort to determine where population expansions occurred in ancient America, a large group of researchers studied the mtDNA of 1612 Native Americas located throughout the United States.[5] The results of the study were published in the February 2002 issue of the *American Journal of Human Genetics*. The authors found that haplogroup X is essentially restricted to two locations in America: in the traditional Iroquois lands and in America's Southwest. Both of these locations are, of course, places where Cayce stated the Atlanteans settled.

While hoping to prove that a single migration could have populated the Americas, the authors concluded that "the early inhabitants of this region [North America] experienced substantial amounts of gene flow." In particular, haplogroup X came in several different waves of migration separated by time. The Southwest experienced an influx of haplogroup X in 10,000 B.C., but it was already present in the area.

Haplogroup X also appeared in the Iroquois lands in the same time periods. In addition, the research discovered one other curious migration into the Iroquois lands. Another influx of haplogroup X came to the Iroquois area in about 1000 B.C. This is especially interesting in light of Cayce's rather specific statements. Haplogroup X may eventually turn out not to be Atlantean mtDNA, but the distribution of it in America and elsewhere, and the migrational chronology genetics researchers have found—exactly fit—what Cayce stated about the Atlantean movements.

Mu Enters The Picture

Cayce used the term *Mu* to describe an area of the South Pacific where a very old and ancient people once lived. The people of Mu were the oldest on earth, but their lands began to break up about 50,000 B.C. The term *Lemuria* is probably more familiar to some readers, but Cayce stated that Lemuria was an island of Mu.

After haplogroup B was initially discovered in Native Americans, it quickly was discovered that haplogroup B was present in areas of China, Southeast Asia, and in the South Pacific. Many geneticists immediately speculated that haplogroup B reached the Americas via water migrations from the South Pacific. But since such a thing was considered impossible, archaeologists countered by asserting that these people simply walked through Siberia across Beringia during the last Ice Age. But more discoveries showed that this wasn't likely, especially since haplogroup B seemed to have arrived in America so early—just after 50,000 B.C. Mainstream belief is now that these ancient people essentially traveled by small boats to America following a "coastal" path. In essence, it is speculated that they first went north, traveling in small boats hugging the Asia coast until they reached Beringia. Then they turned south, following the Pacific Coast. A host of archaeologists are now working at several sites along America's Pacific Coast and also underwater to try to find evidence of this proposed route.

In North America, haplogroup B is virtually confined to the Southwest. The ancient remains of only one individual outside of that regional area have ever been found to be haplogroup B. That individual was found on a mountain in the Northwest. The discovery was of course heralded as "proof" that haplogroup B came across Beringia, but that shaky possibility is now even more unlikely.

Haplogroup B In South America & The South Pacific

As discussed in this chapter, haplogroup B is found in large numbers along the South American Coast. It is also found in the Peruvian Andes, in Bolivia, as well as in Brazil.[3, 4, 5, 6] Thus haplogroup B is confined to southwest America and is essentially densest on the western side of South America. Research shows that haplogroup B seems to have come to America separately—in its own migrational waves—waves that began at least 35,000 years ago and probably much earlier.[7]

The people of the South Pacific are traditionally called the "Oceanic-Speaking Peoples," and the vast region they inhabit is divided into three areas: Polynesia, Micronesia, and Melanesia. Since the 1980s, it has been known that people lived on the islands before 28,000 B.C., but in 28,000 B.C. a large group of people entered the area of Melanesia and "colonized" it.[8]

These accepted facts also perfectly match Cayce's basic story of Mu. When the lands of Mu began to "sink," starting in 50,000 B.C., the people were forced to move to higher ground. According to Cayce, in 28,000 B.C. the same eruptions that devastated Atlantis also devastated Mu. Thus it would be reasonable to expect a large movement of survivors to the remaining "islands"—as well as to other locations. This of course could be the origin of the group that archaeologists know entered Melanesia in 28,000 B.C.

Prior to 2002, it had been assumed that haplogroup B originated in Asia, and that the "Oceanic-Speaking Peoples" of the South Pacific came from Asia also. In fact, the theory holding sway in the field has been that the South Pacific people had migrated from the island of Taiwan long ago.[8]

A 2002 study published in the journal *Genetics*[8] investigated this theory utilizing the Y chromosome of human nDNA (not mitochondrial DNA). The researchers collected human DNA from 390 individuals representing 17 different South Pacific Ocean locations as well as from Taiwan. The unexpected results showed that the largest portion of the people of Polynesia and Melanesia had *not* originated in Taiwan as long suspected. Instead, their origin was cited as an unknown location somewhere "in Melanesia and/or eastern Indonesia." One group in Polynesia shared a chromosomal lineage with the Taiwan sample, but the researchers found that the migration separating these two groups had occurred only 4500 years ago.

In brief, the evidence shows that the ancestors of most of the South Pacific peoples had been there so long that the human DNA indicated that their present location was their place of origin. The implications of this research are clear in regard to Cayce's chronology of Mu. The people of Mu, according to Cayce, were the first people of earth. While the DNA research on the South Pacific peoples doesn't say that they were the oldest people on earth, it can't place their origin anywhere else than where they live right now.

In sum, the distribution of haplogroup B in southwest America and its heavy concentration on the Pacific side of South America is suggestive. Since we also know haplogroup B entered the Americas very early, and we know they focused their settlements to the south, it seems likely their origin was somewhere in the South Pacific—perhaps from an area that has sometimes been called Mu.

In addition, we know that the South Pacific islands were inhabited prior to 28,000 B.C., and that a large migration came to the area in 28,000 B.C. from an unknown area. But since the genetic record—the time machine with which we can look into the past—tells us that the people who migrated to Melanesia in 28,000 B.C. weren't genetically "different" from the people already there, it seems a logical step to speculate that some of their own people entered from adjacent lands. Finally, since we now know that the South Pacific islanders did not come from Asia, we are left with a conclusion that seems to contradict the idea that their ancestors came from Africa. Perhaps the South Pacific islands and the people remaining on them are what Cayce stated they were—the surviving remnants of Mu.

Chapter 5

Legends & Myths
of South America

In prior chapters we've touched on a few myths from South American cultures. There are so many myths from the continent that they sometimes seem to be a bewildering jumble of many stories. Closer examination of these myths reveals that they consist of many versions of the same legends. Consistent among them all is this story, conveying the primary themes from the various tales.

The Ancient Times & Creation

In ancient times the Sun did not exist, and the earth was populated by powerful, primeval beings (presumably akin to the giant, powerful Nephilim in the Western Bible, Genesis 6:4). These ancient beings lost interest in their creator and their divine destiny and became self-seeking, self-gratifying monsters, living increasingly in primitive barbarity. As recorded in Genesis 6:5-7: "Jehovah saw that the wickedness of man was great in the earth, and that every imagination of the thoughts of his heart was only evil continually. And it repented Jehovah that he had made man on the earth, and it grieved him at his heart. And Jehovah said, 'I will destroy man whom I have created from the face of the ground; both man, and beast, and creeping things, and birds of the heavens; for it repenteth me that I have made them.'"

In the South American legends, as in the Western biblical ones, the Creator wiped the Earth clean of these wayward beings by means of a great flood, "higher than the highest mountains," recall the Inca tales of this flood. The only people to survive were a man and a woman who remained in a box and were carried by the wind to Tihuanaco (the abode of the creator). After the waters receded, the creator god made a new race, or in many versions, new races of humans. The creator god first made them out of clay, shaping them into statues and painting them with the colors and clothes of their respective nations. The creator god gave them language, song, and the seeds they were to sow. Then the creator god breathed life into their clay figures and they came alive. The creator god ordered them to pass under the Earth and emerge in the places he directed them. Some came out of caves; others out of hills and cliffs; others from fountains; some from stones; and some from the trunks of trees.

Since it was still dark on the Earth, the creator god created the Sun, moon, and stars and ordered them to go to the island of Titicaca to illuminate the new world.

At this point in the stories, there are various versions of the next stage in creation. Most tell of the Sun, rising into the heavens to bring its light, calling back to the Inca peoples to become lords and leaders to the primitive peoples of the Earth. How these primitive people survived the flood is not explained. The Sun god said to the Inca: "You and your descendants are to be Lords and are to subjugate many nations. Look upon me as your father, and you shall be my children, and you shall

View of Lake Titicaca.
Source: © Philip Baird/www.anthroarcheart.org.

worship me as your father." With these words the Sun gave to the first male leader, Manco Capac, and the first female leader, Mama Ocllo, headdresses and insignias. The Sun god also instructed them to pierce and adorn their ears as the Sun god's ears, were pierced, with golden earrings.

Some versions of this story describe how in ancient times there were three small openings to a deep cave (or on the side of a high cliff) called *Tambotocco*, meaning "Place of the Hole." In some versions there were three small exits out of an ancient wayside lodging called *Paccari-tambo*, meaning "Inn of Origin." Through the middle opening of these three holes, or exits, came the original royal founders of the Inca. They scared away or conquered without violence (a unique aspect of South American tales) the primitive peoples in the surrounding areas and established the city of Cuzco, whose name means "the navel." Some legends say the ancient openings into this world are above or under Lake Titicaca. The first rulers or leaders are almost always Manco Capac and his wife and sister, Mama Ocllo. Manco Capac goes northward to gather his followers and bring them to Cuzco. Mama Ocllo goes southward to gather her followers and bring them to Cuzco. (Adapted from Molina, 1573.)

The Sun God Among the People

In various versions the Sun god takes the place of or replaces the creator god or is somehow a projection of a portion of the creator god into the lives of humans on Earth. This individualized manifestation of god among the people comes in various names: Thunupa or Pachacamac, but the most widely used name is Viracocha.

Sulistani burial chambers at Lake Titicaca. Source: © Philip Baird/ www.anthroarcheart.org.

The legends surrounding Viracocha are similar in many ways to Maya and Aztec legends of a man-like god who came among them and then left, promising to return. According to the South American versions, Viracocha was a bearded white man who came up from the south. Pedro de Cieza de Leon records in his *Cronica del Peru*, written in 1553, this legend told to him by the indigenous peoples: "Before the Incas ruled or had even been heard of in these kingdoms, these Indians relate a thing more noteworthy than anything else that they say. They assert that they were a long time without seeing the Sun; and suffering much hardship from this, they offered prayers and vows to those whom they held for gods, beseeching them to give what they lacked. At this the Sun very brilliant rose from the island of Titicaca in the great lake of the Collao, and all were rejoiced. After this had happened they say that there suddenly appeared, coming from the south, a white man of large stature and authoritative demeanor. This man had such great power that he changed the hills into valleys and from valleys made great hills, causing streams to flow from the living stone. When they saw his power they called him 'Maker of All Things Created' and 'Prince of All Things,' 'Father of the Sun.' For he did other still more wonderful things, giving being to men and animals; in a word by his hand very great benefits accrued to them. This is the story that the Indians themselves told me

Pre-Inca ruins at Pachacamac.
Source: © Philip Baird/www.anthroarcheart.org.

and they heard it from their fathers who in their turn had it from the old songs which were handed down from very ancient times.

"They say that this man traveled along the highland route to the north, working marvels as he went and that they never saw him again. They say that in many places he gave men instructions how they should live, speaking to them with great love and kindness and admonishing them to be good and to do no damage or injury one to another, but to love one another and show charity to all. In most places they named him Ticci Viracocha, but in the province of Collao he is called Tuapaca (Thunupa) or in some parts of it, Arunaua. In many places they build temples to him and in them they set up statues in his likeness and offered sacrifices before them. The huge statues in the village of Tiahuanaco are held to be from those times." (From Part II, chapters 4 and 5.)

Views of Inca ruins at Pisac. Source: *Corel.*

The indigenous people also told Cieza de Leon that some time after the disappearance of Viracocha, a similar man was seen, who healed the sick and restored sight to the blind using only his words. Legends tell that as he was approaching the village of Cacha, the people rose up to stone him. As they drew near, he knelt down and raised his eyes to the heavens, and a great fire appeared in the sky. They became afraid and asked him to forgive them. He did, but the heat of the fire was so great that the stones in the surrounding area became as light as cork. From Cacha he traveled throughout the surrounding areas. In one town he visited a wedding and was refused food and water; for this he turned the wedding party into stone. Rock outcrops in the highland areas are said to be these stingy wedding revelers of ancient times. Eventually, this strange and miraculous man traveled to the seashore, where he spread out his cloak upon the waves and floated away, never to be seen again.

Cieza de Leon records (Part I, chapters 87 and 105) that many of the most ancient and largest buildings in the areas of Guamanga (now Ayacucho) and Vinaque were said to have been built by pre-Inca white people with beards. "When the Indians of the district are asked who made these ancient monuments they reply that they were made by other people, bearded and white like ourselves, who came to that region and settled there many ages before the reign of the Incas. These and

Views of Inca ruins at Olantambo. Source: *Corel.*

some other ancient buildings in this area seem to me to be of a different style of architecture from the buildings which were put up by order of the Inca; for these are square while the Inca buildings are long and narrow. There is also a rumor that an inscription was found on a tile from these buildings. I neither affirm this nor do I abandon my belief that in the distant past there immigrated into this region a people with sufficient intelligence and judgment to have made these things and others which are no longer to be seen."

Just as the Aztecs initially believed that the Spanish Conquistadors were the return of a legendary, bearded, white teacher, so the Inca initially believed the Spanish to be "viracocha," gods. The Conquistadors were received with open arms and veneration. But their greed and brutality soon convinced the Incas to reclassify them as "devils."

The Anti-Viracocha

A fascinating legend among the South American peoples seems to warn of an anti-Sun god, an anti-Viracocha—and the Conquistadors may well have been these evil ones. The story goes that Inca divine kinship was originally established by a profound deception committed by one of the early kings, who dressed himself in a "Shining Mantle" of gold, beads, and jewels. Parading before his ignorant subjects, so

Inca ruins at Tambo Colorado. Source: © Philip Baird/www.anthroarcheart.org.

impressed by his majesty and glittering reflections of sunlight off his cap, they began to worship him as the Sun god, or an offspring of the Sun god. He was a greater deceiver. Similar in many ways to the anti-Christ in the Revelation and the false or foreign god in the Book of Daniel, he deceived the people and led them away from truth. Some versions of the legend associate the deceiver with Sinchi Roca, an Inca monarch, and credit his mother with the trickery. Other versions weave this deceiver idea into stories that the indigenous peoples came from three primordial brothers and three primordial sisters (sometimes the number is four each). Among these ancient brothers, one becomes the deceiver of the people; most reveal him to be the great Manco Capac, despite recounted achievements in other legends. It is said that Manco Capac hammered two plates out of silver, putting one on his chest and the other on his back. Then he climbed the mountain and told the people to watch him as he walked upon the mountain, claiming that they would see that he was now son of the Sun. With the sunlight flashing off of his plates, he appeared to send light out from himself, as does the Sun, and many believed him and gave him anything he wished. (Adapted from Gavilan, 1621, and Montesino.)

The Cross-bearing, Blue-eyed Preacher

In many of these ancient myths, Viracocha rightly overshadows and consumes all other hero legends. However, if one takes the time to carefully separate a specific character who goes by various names—Thunupa, Tonapa, and Taapac, but most commonly the name Thunupa—we discover a fascinating story that surprisingly parallels Western biblical imagery and legend. Furthermore, it is possible that these stories of Thunupa are those of the unnamed healer who returned in the likeness of Viracocha. We find most of the story of Thunupa recounted in Antonio de la Calancha's *Cronica moralizada del orden de San Agustin en el Peru*, published in 1638.

Thunupa came out of the north, where Viracocha had disappeared some time before. He was wearing a rough-cloth, sleeveless shirt from his shoulders to his knees and carrying a large wooden cross on his back! He had blue eyes, a beard, austere physique, and a solemn manner. He preached against violence and excesses of pleasures, including substance abuse, sexual promiscuity, and polygamy.

In *Account of the Antiquities of Peru*, Salcamaychua reports this description of Thunupa: "In those days the *curacas* [village leader] of Asillu and Hucuru told the Inca how in ancient times a poor thin old man with a beard and long hair had come to them in a long tunic and that he was a wise counselor in matters of state and that his name was Thunupa Vihinquira. They said that he had banished all the idols and Hapi-fluflu demons to the snowy mountains." The account goes on to explain that human sacrifice had begun as a result of the negative influences of the idols and Hapi-fluflu upon the people and their lives. This banishment by order of Thunupa Vihinquira ended the human sacrifice.

In other accounts of the Thunupa, it is said that he was not popular among all the people. He criticized the famed monarch Makuri of the city of Carapucu for his cruelty and warring. In the city of Sicasica, his preaching aggravated the population so much that they set fire to the house in which he was sleeping. He escaped without harm.

Upon returning to Carapucu it is said that one of King Makuri's daughters had fallen in love with one of Thunupa's disciples (he had arrived in the area bringing five disciples with him). The disciple had converted the daughter, and Thunupa had baptized her into their faith. This angered Makuri so much that he had his men kill the disciple and Thunupa. The disciple died, but Thunupa was unconscious and near dead. Calancha recounts what happened next:

"They put his blessed body in a boat of totora rush [rushes found around Lake Titicaca and used to make waterproof boats] and set it adrift on Lake Titicaca. There the gentle waters served him oars and the soft winds for pilot, and he sailed away with such speed that

Closeup of Tiahuanaco's Gate of the Sun. Many people believe the image represents Thunupa. Source: *Wonders of the Past* (1923).

those who had tried so cruelly to kill him were left behind in terror and astonishment. For the lake has no current. ... The boat came to the shore at Cochamarca, where today is the river Desaguadero. Indian tradition asserts that the boat struck the land with such force it created the river Desaguadero, which before then did not exist. Released on the water, the holy body was carried many leagues away to the sea coast at Arica." Thunupa was never seen again. However, Salcamayhua reveals that the Inca still had some among them that worshiped Thunupa near the place where he first arrived, conducting ceremonies that resembled baptisms, pouring water over babies, while celebrating the praises of Thunupa.

A fascinating part of the Thunupa legend recounts how some of those who opposed Thunupa attempted to destroy his wooden cross by chopping it into pieces and burning it. But according to the legend, they were unable to cut into it with their blades or to set it aflame. They even tried to sink it in the great lake at Titicaca, but it wouldn't sink! They then buried it. According to Ramos Gavilan's *Historia del celebre y milagroso Santuario de la insigne imagen de Nuestra Senora de Copacabana,* published in 1621, the buried cross was later found by the Augustine Fathers in 1569!

The Giants

Ancient giants are a common feature in myth and legend throughout the world. The Greek author Philostratus (c. 218 A.D.) wrote that it was logical to accept that "giants once existed, because their awesome remains could be seen all around the world." The Greek geographer Pausanias wrote about the excitement that surrounded the supposed discovery of the bones of the great Greek champion Ajax. An eyewitness explained how the sea had washed out the beach, revealing a pile of giant bones: "Ajax's kneecaps were exactly the size of a discus for the boy's pentathlon," wrote Pausanias. A boy's discus was about six inches across. Giants may have existed in the Miocene era (approximately 8 million years ago) in which the fossil remains of mastodons, mammoths, giant giraffes, rhinoceroses, cave bears, and other gigantic animals have been found in the eastern Mediterranean region, where these tales originate.

In Genesis the giant Nephilim are mentioned as existing prior to the great flood of Noah. They were powerful, god-like beings that became so corrupt that God regretted having made them.

A quasi-biblical text, fragments of which were found among the Dead Sea scrolls, is titled *The Book of Giants*. It is composed in Syriac, an Eastern dialect of Aramaic. The book was unknown until the finding of the Dead Sea scrolls, although references to it survived in Latin, Greek, and Arabic, indicating that it recorded battles among ancient giants.

Two of the giants in the the book are named Gilgamesh and Hobabis. Gilgamesh is an epic figure in Sumerian and Akkadian literature, best known from the "Epic of Gilgamesh," an ancient Mesopotamian tale comparable to that of the Homeric epics in ancient Greece. According to the Epic, Gilgamesh, a huge semi-divine man, has many adventures with his friend, the wild man Enkidu. One of these adventures reports the slaying of the monster Humbaba (Huwawa) in the Cedar Forest. But Enkidu dies tragically, and Gilgamesh sets out to discover the secret of immortality in order to avoid his friend's fate. He meets Utnapishtim, the Babylonian version of Noah—the only man to survive the Flood. Unlike Noah, Utnapishtim was made immortal by the gods. Nevertheless, Gilgamesh fails in his quest, eventually dying and leaving only his heroic fame behind him.

The Hebrew manuscript *Midrash of Shemihazah* tells how at the time of the corrupt generation of the Flood, the angels Shemihazah and Aza'el make a bet with God that if they were to descend from heaven to earth they would be able to resist the lure of evil. But after descending, they promptly lose the bet as they become enchanted by the beauty of mortal women and cannot restrain themselves from becoming sexually involved with them. Soon they find themselves revealing heavenly secrets to their mortal wives. Shemihazah begets sons named Heyya and Aheyya. The angel Metatron (another name for the deified Enoch in the Hekhalot traditions) sends them a warning of the coming Flood. Heyya and Aheyya each have a prophetic dream. In the first, an angel descends from heaven and scrapes an enormous stone tablet with writing on it. It is then spread across the whole world until only four words remain. In the second, there is a garden full of trees and gems, but an angel descends and cuts down everything but one tree with three branches. Both dreams predict the coming of the Flood, and the destruction of all human beings except

Noah and his three sons. The giants are then killed in the Flood but are consoled by the fact that mortals will use their names in incantations; thus their fame will never cease. Shemihazah repents and suspends himself upside down between heaven and earth. Aza'el refuses to repent and becomes a demon, who entices men to do corrupt deeds and who bears the sins of Israel on the Day of Atonement (see Lev. 16:7-10).

Recently many fragments of Manichean works written in Central Asian languages were recovered archaeologically at Turfan, in China. As in the previous two stories, a Sogdian text of the Manichean version refers to Atanbush, who is either another giant or Enoch himself, under another name. (Enoch also survived the Flood and was made immortal.) Atanbush conducts himself in exactly the same manner as Utnapishtim in *The Book of Giants*. To have such similar stories found around the world makes it difficult to toss out all giant legends as figments of primitive, human imagination.

Among the South American legends is the tale of giants who came to the shores of the pre-Incan lands from far away. These giants are said to have landed in giant boats at Santa Helena, near Puerto Viejo. A full-grown, normal human standing next to these giants would only come up to their knees! They had no beards, long hair down to their shoulders, and wore animal skins or nothing at all. According to the legend, they had no females with them, and none of the local women would have anything to do them. They built deep wells into solid rock. Salcamayhua writes the following account: "In these wells there is excellent and wholesome water, so cool that it is always a delight to drink." He goes on to tell that though the giants created a source for water, they did nothing to create a food supply, eating up the whole countryside. They also killed men and women for various reasons, most unjustified. The people joined together to resist these giants but could do nothing to stop them. Many years went by with these giants in their lands. But the legends tell of how God intervened, mostly in reaction to the lewd and perverted sexual activity of these giants. A "fearful and terrifying fire came down from the sky with a huge noise and from the midst came forth a shining angel, a sharp and glittering sword in his hand. With a single blow he slew them all and the fire consumed them, so that there remained only a few bones and skulls which God permitted to stay unconsumed by the fire as a memory of this punishment."

The Spanish report that they found huge human bones, and human teeth weighing half a pound each!

The Ethereal Ones

The peoples that lived along the coastal lands of South America have a tale that fits quite well with Edgar Cayce's reports of semi-physical beings of great power living in the ancient times. They were originally co-creators with the great Creator, but eventually lost harmony with the Most High Creator and were destroyed or transformed; after which the true Creator recreated life anew.

Francisco Lopez de Gomara recounts in his *Historia General de las Indias* (Chapter 122) the following tale of a boneless, pre-Inca being who created much of the land and life that was found in these parts when the Inca arrived. "They say that at the beginning of the world there came from the north a man called Con, who was without bones. He was quick and agile and journeyed far. He eased his path by lowering the mountains and raising the valleys simply by the power of his will and word, as became the child of the Sun, which he declared himself to be. He filled the land with men and women whom he created, and gave them much fruit and bread and the other necessities of life. Nevertheless, because some of them caused him annoyance, he turned the good land he had given them into dry and barren deserts, like those that are by the coast, and caused the rain to cease so that from that time it has not rained in those parts. He left them only the rivers in his clemency that they might support themselves by irrigation and toil."

Lopez de Gomara goes on to say, "There next came Pachacamac [*pacha*, 'the world;' and *camac*, 'creator'], also son of the Sun and Moon, and he drove out Con and changed his men into monkeys, after which he created anew the men and women who exist today and furnished them with all the things they have. In gratitude for such benefits, they made him their god and used to worship him at Pachacamac [a site of the most renowned pre-Inca temples, near the modern city of Lima], until such time as the Christians came and cast him out of there, whereat they were much astonished. The temple of Pachacamac near Lima was most celebrated in those lands and was much frequented for worship and for its oracles, for the devil would appear and used to converse with the priests who lived there. [Remember, a Spanish Christian is writing this account of the indigenous people's legend. His prejudice is evident.] The Spanish who went there with Hernando Pizarro after the capture of Atabaliba robbed it of all its gold and silver and then brought to an end the visions and oracles with the coming of the cross, a thing which caused the Indians horror and alarm."

So revered was Pachacamac, and his temple so majestic and sacred, that the Incas, who built temples to the Sun everywhere they went, did not dare to defile Lima's Pachacamac temple for fear that the people would never cooperate. Instead, they agreed to the continuance of worship to Pachacamac on condition that a temple to the Sun would be set on a high piece of land nearby.

Legend has it that even before the Spanish governor heard of this temple and its great wealth, and sent his brother, Hernando Pizarro, to rob it of its treasures, the indigenous peoples had already carried away four hundred loads of gold before he arrived! Lopez de Gomara wrote that the four hundred loads have not been discovered and that "the Indians alive today don't know where it is."

Consistent Themes In South American Myths & Legends

When one considers the myths and legends of the indigenous peoples of South America, recurring themes emerge:

1. A great flood separating two creations is described by virtually all the South American myths. The flood destroys nearly all humanity or the vast majority of it. Survivors of the flood had fled to the Andes, centering in the area of Cuzco and Lake Titicaca.

2. The first creation included the Creator God, god-like beings who initially helped humanity live better, and also rogue beings of great power (semi-divine, such as Con). These rogue beings had great stature and strength (giants) that terrorized the people and the lands.

3. The second creation was performed by the "Creator of the World," producing a new race or several races of peoples. This creation began well, but because of human mistakes and selfish, pleasure-seeking attitudes, it ended in hardship and toil, requiring constant supplication to God and the gods for help and forgiveness.

4. There were many traveling people in very ancient times. The myths mainly record significant events by individuals or small groups

of people, but also relate that some larger groups moved into the continent.

5. Prior to the Great Flood, the myths tell that the visitors came from the south and headed north. After the Great Flood they apparently came from both the north and south.

6. When the Spanish arrived in the 1500s, the indigenous peoples were found to be healthy and wealthy; organized into stratified cultures with communities and large cities; and had adequate food, shelter, clothing, and water. They had many sacred sites and were receiving divine guidance via oracle-like communications in their temples (in a manner similar to the Jews in the Holy of Holies and the Greeks at Delphi). There was animal and grain sacrifice, as in the Jewish temple, with occasional human sacrifice.

7. The very early myths, as well as archaeological evidence, indicate that the first offerings in temple sacrifices were probably sacred objects such as rock crystal or feathers. Gradually, human sacrifice entered into the rituals.

8. The indigenous peoples had encountered traveling white people with blue eyes long before the Spanish arrived. These visitors appear to have arrived in at least two separate eras. Some of their legends date the white visitor(s) to the age before the Great Flood (Viracocha and the one who returned in his likeness); some after the Flood (Thunupa and five disciples). These myths closely parallel the myths of the Aztec and Maya of Mexico.

Mythology & Cayce

In *The Lost Hall of Records* (2000), Cayce's story of humanity is summarized. According to Cayce, there have been four different creations of life, which he occasionally refers to as "root races." The first two root races developed 10-12 million years ago in the South Pacific land of Mu. These early life forms were quite primitive and did not have conscious awareness in the same way as modern man. Nor were these early life forms truly human. The third root race began in Atlantis in about 106,000 B.C. and was a much-improved physical form.

In 50,700 B.C. a series of disturbances on earth began to break up both Atlantis and Mu, causing a migration to higher ground and safer places. A second set of physical disturbances occurred in 28,000

B.C., causing near-complete devastation in Mu and Atlantis. A great flood then transpired, leading to the deaths of the vast majority of human life.

In Cayce's chronology the fourth root race began about 12,000 B.C., with the simultaneous appearance of modern man in five separate locations. The red race appeared in the remnants of Atlantis; the white race appeared in the Caucus Mountains; the black race appeared in Nubia; the yellow race appeared in the Gobi; and the brown race appeared in the remnants of Mu (including both the Andes and the South Pacific).

Consistent with Cayce's chronology, the earliest South American myths relate the story of a great flood that destroyed nearly all life in the continent. There are tales of giant humans and people with great power. The myths also parallel the biblical story of the Flood, but Lake Titicaca and Cuzco figure heavily in the South American version. The story also seems to be related to the myth of the origin of the Inca. In that story it seems that some sort of catastrophic event may have blotted out the sun or greatly darkened the skies. A small group of people—all of whom were genetically related to each other—came into the Cuzco/Titicaca area and established a higher level of civilization. With the first appearance of these people, the sun began shining again, the indigenous peoples attributing this wondrous event to the newcomers. The Inca myths—in some ways—reveal that they were chosen ones, selected by god to rule over the land.

In sum, the myths from South America reveal that the land was settled in very remote times—a story that seems to be fully borne out by the archaeological record. The myths tell that various groups of people entered from both the north and south, as well as across water from those directions. Genetic research and information from traditional archaeological work seems to support this aspect of the story. The myths also relate that small groups of people came into the Andes in quite remote times. These people were more advanced than the people already living in the area, and the newcomers gradually became the dominant culture. The known facts about the Inca, the relatively small group of people who gradually came to dominate and subjugate all of the other major South American cultures, appear to be the source of this myth.

Chapter 6

The Fringe World of South American Archaeology:
Big Balls, Balloons, & Tunnel Complexes

South America contains many genuine mysteries and each and every one of them has had numerous books and articles published about them. These books have raised the public's awareness of South America but have also created some strange ideas. In this chapter our hope is to simply touch base with a few of these ideas and summarize the current beliefs held by Latin American archaeologists about them.

Costa Rica's Balls

Quite a bit has been written about the mysterious stone spheres that have been found in Costa Rica (in Central America). A handful of fairly recent authors take credit for "discovering" some of them, but the actual discovery goes back to a much earlier time.

In 1940 the United Fruit Company began clearing dense sections of Costa Rican jungle to plant trees. During this process their workers began uncovering buried or partially buried solid stone spheres. Some of these stone balls were huge, measuring up to seven feet in diameter and weighing more than 16 tons. The first archaeological report published on them was in 1943, when Costa Rican archaeologists reported finding pottery and other artifacts associated with the spheres.

Several thousand balls—all made from hand-polished granite—have been found in a fairly wide-ranging area in river beds and ancient burial sites in southwest Costa Rica and also on Caño Island, lying some nine miles off the coast. The smallest ball is about the size of an orange. All of them had been quarried and polished to a near-perfect spherical shape. Costa Rica's balls are completely unique—similar objects have not been found anywhere else in the world.

Few of the stone balls remain in their original locations, and some of the largest were simply dynamited, because moving them proved to be too difficult and expensive for the land clearers. It appears that most—if not all—of the "new" discoveries of the balls are simply a rediscovery of a ball that was obscurely known or had been moved.

The stone balls are truly mysterious. Their uniqueness—near-perfect shape, enormous size, and the sheer number of them—is amazing. Where they were quarried is known but how the gigantic ones were moved the 50 miles or so to the coastal area isn't clear. One could venture a reasonable guess on the method of transportation based on their shape (they were probably rolled), but it obviously took a lot of preparation and work to do so.

Costa Rican balls in the Boruco Region. Source: *Handbook of South American Indians* (1948), Bureau of Ethnology, U.S. Gov. Printing Office.

The biggest mystery about the stone balls lies in their purpose. Many of them were associated with burials, and Costa Rican archaeologists take the view that they were created by the Chibcha Culture, which erected fortified cities on the coast. Exactly why the balls were created isn't explained by identifying their makers. Others have speculated that the balls were placed in a pattern to represent constellations or to perhaps create some sort of path. The bottom line is that all of these ideas are just interesting speculations, because we just don't know the answers.

How Were the Nazca Lines Planned and Sighted?

As discussed in a prior chapter, the Nazca lines are a genuine mystery. The manner in which the lines were constructed, however, is not a mystery. The lines were made by removing the surface layer of the desert floor, exposing a different colored layer below it. The top layer was piled along the sides of the lines with surface stones to create defined edges for the continuous lines that form the figures. However, because some of the figures are so incredibly large—essentially perfect depictions of rather intricate life forms—there is no way that the people directing the work could have accomplished that task from ground level.

While some have suggested that vantage points on mountains were utilized by those overseeing the work, that simply wasn't possible for the most intricate forms. They can't be seen from any mountains. Thus the wildest speculation is that aliens hovering in space ships directed the workers.

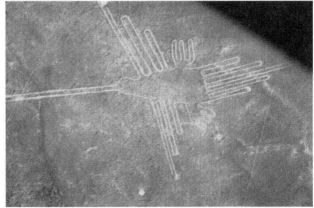

The Hummingbird at Nazca. Source: © Philip Baird/ www.anthroarcheart.org.

The most plausible explanation does involve an aerial view, but a view from a hovering or stationary platform. Thus a handful of people suspected that the Nazca people might have used some form of hot-air balloon, and a team of Americans all but proved it in the 1970s.

The Cayce readings make frequent mention of the Atlanteans' flying technology. They had hot-air balloons, craft that are described as similar to blimps, and even more advanced aircraft, though nothing like the ability to fly into space is mentioned. The Cayce readings relate that Atlanteans carried the knowledge of such technology with them when some migrated to the Andes area in 10,000 B.C. and even before that time.

One unexplained aspect of the Nazca lines that had been noted by both visitors and archaeologists alike was the presence of ancient "burn pits" within some of the intricate figures as well as at other places between the lines. In addition, in historic times, tribes in Guatemala, El Salvador, and Peru had been observed making and "launching smoke balloons" as part of religious ceremonies. The balloons traditionally were made from dried animal intestines that were carefully sewn together. The combination of these two observations led to a startling speculation—the ancient people of Nazca may have utilized hot-air balloons to direct the layout of the lines.

In the early 1970s a small group of Americans from the International Explorers Society began investigating the hot-air-balloon theory. The Explorers first reviewed ancient legends, texts, and cave paintings from around the world, finding a rich history of man's fascination with flying and hints that some people had actually experienced flight. They believed they had found tantalizing evidence indicating that some ancient cultures had probably developed primitive,

The Spider at Nazca.
Source: © Philip Baird/
www.anthroarcheart.org.

hot-air balloons. In addition, they found Inca legends describing what seemed to be flying in balloons.

Next, the burn pits within the lines were thoroughly investigated, leading them to the conclusion that they were used several times but within a small time frame. In addition, they found that the extent and size of the fires seemed to be ideal for launching hot-air balloons and keeping them aloft. But they had no idea what materials could have been used in the construction of ancient balloons.

In 1973 they were notified that a variety of samples of ancient textiles had been discovered in a 1500-year-old grave site at Nazca along with pottery and other artifacts. The Explorers managed to obtain several samples of the textiles from a grave robber at the site. The man told them that a number of large, cotton "bed sheets" were found in burial pots associated with mummies at the site. The group was subsequently taken to an extensive Nazca burial area (1000 years old) located on private land. The area was covered with sand dunes. Under the dunes they found adobe brick burial temples. They immediately found a skull and pottery, but what caught their attention was a burial sack. Inside the sack they found a white fabric resembling a modern bed sheet. It was of a dense weave, "more dense than cotton shirts." The torn fabric was four feet long and six inches wide.

As they continued their walk through the graves, pieces of similar fabric were found everywhere, scattered among pottery, skulls, bones, and adobe tombs. The grave robber eventually told the Explorers that he had once found a carved stone at Nazca that he and his friends came

to call the "potato," because the carving looked like a large potato with a very small basket under it. He related that he had sold the stone some years earlier in Lima.

The next piece of evidence coming to the Explorers was completely unexpected. They received three old stamps issued by the Brazilian government to commemorate the first balloon flight. But

Nazca mummy. Source:
© Philip Baird/
www.anthroarcheart.org.

the stamps didn't honor the "first" balloon flight listed in the encyclopedias, a 1783 hot-air balloon flight by a Frenchman. Instead, one of the stamps, issued in 1944, was in honor of de Gusmão, who had supposedly launched a hot-air balloon in 1709, as were the other two stamps. The Explorers were astonished and could not believe what they were seeing.

The 1944 stamp displayed a painting of a white fabric balloon launched with a small basket under it. It looked like a white potato with a small basket attached to its bottom. De Gusmão is not credited in any American or European texts for his feat, but a statue of him was erected in Santos in 1913, where it remains today. In fact, the statue is the centerpiece of a large plaza decorated with depictions of ancient and historic balloons. Following up on clues obtained from inscriptions around the statue, the Explorers found a 1917 Swiss pamphlet describing the 1709 balloon flight. Then the archives at the Vatican found a copy of Gusmão's petition to the King of Portugal in 1709, asking for permission to fly his new craft.

A little later, the Explorers obtained a French book detailing Gusmão's appearance before the King wherein he was described as carrying a small cotton-fabric balloon. The King granted him permission to fly, and after returning to Brazil, he took his balloon to a height of 60 feet. The Explorers believe that Gusmão got the idea from Inca legends that describe a form of hovering flight craft. Despite this set of facts, the first balloon flight is still credited to France in 1783.

After obtaining official permission from Brazilian authorities, the Explorer team constructed a sewn, cotton-fabric balloon, duplicating the textiles that had been found at the Nazca graves. On a specially designated site on the Nazca Desert, they built a fire pit identical to the ones found between the Nazca lines. The first two attempts to launch the fabric balloon were aborted, because the Explorers didn't know how to control the heat of the fire. But by the third attempt, they easily mastered the problem and launched their balloon—named Condor I. The balloon was tethered to the ground and suspended 400 feet above the desert floor for five minutes with two team members onboard. As the balloon began to cool and descend, they managed to keep it hovering by throwing sand ballasts over the sides of the small reed basket under the balloon. After nearly 10 minutes, the balloon settled to the desert floor. Everyone was jubilant as the two occupants of the basket jumped out, causing the balloon to quickly shoot up to 1200 feet, pulling the stakes from the ground as it was carried off by the wind. Over 1000 people were present for the event, including a large media group, and they watched as the balloon drifted for miles at a height of 1000 feet.

The Explorers' balloon was recovered and placed in the National Aeronautical Museum in Lima. In response to questions asked by media who recorded the event at Nazca, the story of Viracocha was recounted. "He ascended into the sky after having finished making all that is in the land." The Nazca lines, the Explorers contended, had been made by people who knew how to make and use hot-air balloons. The knowledge was lost with the deaths of specific people, but the legends retell the story.[1]

Gigantic Tunnels & Chambers

South American stories tell of the existence of huge tunnels and complexes of rooms and chambers carved into the mountains. The Spanish were extremely interested in the stories, because vast amounts of gold and silver were said to have been hidden in them. As we have seen, many pyramids in South America were honeycombed with tunnels and tomb chambers packed with gold and other precious artifacts. Few of the pyramids have actually been excavated, and it is highly likely that enormous amounts of gold and silver will eventually be found within them.

As discussed earlier, the Inca road system was carved from stone, and in many places short tunnels were constructed. In addition, the collapsed rubble of countless tunnel entrances is found nearly everywhere in South America. Because of the danger posed, governments closed off some of the tunnels, but others appear to have fallen during earthquakes.

Perhaps the most intriguing tales of lost tunnels were related by Harold T. Wilkins in his 1946 book, *Mysteries of Ancient South America*. Wilkins came to believe that an underground tunnel went from Lima to Cuzco—a distance of some 400 miles—mostly through the Andes. According to Wilkins, that wasn't the longest tunnel, because another one extended 900 miles to the south, ending at Salar de Atacama. The theosophist Madame Blavatsky also became convinced that tunnels existed in South America. When she visited the continent, she obtained a map of the entire tunnel system from a native at Lima. The map is kept at the Theosophical Society headquarters in India.

Legends also tell of massive tunnels in Chile and smaller ones throughout the entire continent. In addition, the series of books written about the continent of Mu by James Churchward in the 1920s and 1930s is based, in part, on artifacts supposedly found in large tunnels and chambers. Few archaeologists accept any of these artifacts as genuine, yet there are thousands of them, and they do, in fact, appear to be ancient. Those interested in reading a wide range of these fantastic tales are referred to Childress' *Lost Cities and Ancient Mysteries of South America.*[2]

What sense can be made out of these stories and tales of tunnels? First, the legends appear to be based on fact. There were tunnels that held riches in South America, and some are being explored by archaeologists today. Tunnels in the huge pyramids often led to a honeycomb of chambers and tombs containing gold. Secondly, the Inca constructed tunnels for their extensive road system. In addition, ancient mine tunnels were dug in many places in South America from which gold and silver deposits were removed. Some of these mine tunnels were quite deep and long, but few of them can be explored today. It is also likely that as the Spanish moved through South America, the Inca rulers hid quantities of gold within the mountains, exactly as numerous legends and stories recount.

The stories telling of tunnels that are secret passages to remote locations may also be based in fact. Many mountains in America have cave systems that extend hundreds of miles, with multiple entrances. For example, Mammoth Cave in Kentucky has over 365 miles of passages already mapped, and experts have no idea where it ends. Lechugilla Cave at Carlsbad has been traced thus far for 98 miles, with the ends not yet reached. In Brazil over 500 caves and extensive cave systems are found in the Paraña area. Peru is filled with caves. It is more than likely that there are numerous, undiscovered, giant cave systems in many parts of South America—especially in the Andes. The Inca and those who preceded them may have taken advantage of some of these extensive caves for both travel and storage—or hiding—precious materials. It is likely that they also used their knowledge of mining to make the cave tunnels more passable, even extending them in some places. Such possibilities seem to have been the likely basis for the many tales of hundreds of miles-long tunnels in South America.

Chapter 7

Edgar Cayce and the Unknown History of South America

Among the most fascinating of the 14,000 Edgar Cayce readings are several that review the history of humanity since the beginning of creation.[1] Tantalizing bits and pieces of information about the past can also be found woven throughout the texts of Cayce's past life readings. For example, over 650 people were given detailed descriptions of lives they had lived thousands, and even millions of years ago, during the time of the legendary civilizations of Lemuria and Atlantis. Seventy-three individuals were told of past lives lived in South America which, according to the readings, was once part of the landmass that comprised Lemuria.[2] This means, of course, that Cayce's history of South America is much more ancient than science has so far been able to determine.

The story revealed in the readings is so compelling and consistent that it has been compiled and studied by several Cayce researchers.[3-5] Although there is a wealth of detail contained in these readings, the chronology is often hard to follow. Specific dates, some of which refer to points in time many thousands of years ago, are provided in only in a few cases. However, there are some specific chronological reference points in the readings that can be used to map out Cayce's version of human history and, more specifically for our purposes, that of South America.

Chronological Reference Points

The first reference point is the time period after the Creation of the earth when the first human civilization, Mu or Lemuria, flourished.

Although the readings don't give an exact date for the first arrival of human beings on earth, they do tell us that 10,500,000 years ago there were 133,000,000 people on the earth. At that time 44 representatives from locations all around the world, including present day Peru, gathered to transcribe the "first laws."[6] In 200,000 B.C. a civilization rose in Atlantis that was impacted by a major geologic catastrophe in 50,722 B.C.[7] This same event may have also caused the demise of much of Lemuria.[8] Two additional catastrophes rocked Altantis in about 28,000 and 10,000 B.C.[9] [10]

The readings also indicate indirectly that *ca.* 12,000 B.C., the five races of man (black, brown, white, red, and yellow) appeared simultaneously in modern human form in five different areas of the earth.[11] [12] Another dating clue in the Cayce readings concerns the time period roughly from 10,600 to 10,400 BC during the lifetime of a Priest in Egypt named Ra Ta. This individual traveled around the world and brought together representatives from all nations to create a compilation of the world's greatest spiritual teachings. The readings also said that he was involved in building the monuments on the Giza Plateau.[13]

Many of the South American past life readings contain the reference points mentioned above and can therefore be roughly dated. In addition, a review of lives mentioned before and after each South American lifetime is also helpful in identifying time periods. Using these methods the following story emerges which reveals a surprisingly extensive history for South America that is both dynamic and ancient.

10,500,000 B.C.
The First Humans in Lemuria and South America

Scientists have estimated that the earth is approximately 4 billion years old.[14] Although the Cayce readings do not provide a specific date for the creation, they do indicate that shortly thereafter a special type of human being began to inhabit the earth. As the readings explain it, these beings were more ethereal at first and did not have true material bodies. Later, the readings say, they occupied temporary, yet physical, hominid-type bodies out of which they could easily remove themselves.[15]

Over a long span of time they eventually reached a point where they were so connected to the material world that death became the only way they could separate from their physical bodies. These first "incarnations," as the readings term them, happened on a large landmass the readings called Lemuria or Mu. This land was also called La or Lamu in the early days when the ethereal beings were first materializing into human forms.[16]

South America: The Western-most Portion of Lemuria

According to the Edgar Cayce readings portions of the South American continent—the Pacific coast around the Peruvian Andes area—existed during the time frame of the Lemurian civilization. In fact, Cayce stated that this area constituted "the extreme western portion of Lemuria."[17]

In addition, the northwestern boundary of Lemuria appears to have extended into the Southwestern United States. One person was told that drawings she had made in a previous lifetime, as a Lemurian *ca.* 10 million B.C., could still be found today in the "ruins...mounds, and caves" of northwestern New Mexico.[18]

Eastern Lemuria extended into the South Pacific and the Gobi in China before it gradually "began its disappearance."[19] The Gobi is referred to in the readings as "the land of Mu" and is described as having risen to a level of "the highest state of advancement in material accomplishments." This group had the ability to use "Flax, cotton, ramie, silk...metals – gold, silver, lead, radium" which continued until the time of Ra Ta (*ca.* 10,500 B.C.) The leader of the Gobi area journeyed to other lands during this time and interacted with representatives from Og (South America).[20]

The Worldwide Gathering of the 44

A ruler from Egypt and a priest from "the land of many waters" (Tibet) gathered together 44 individuals from locations around the world including Mongolia, Caucasia, Norway, the southern cordilleras (Sierra Mountains of Mexico?), Peru, and parts of present day Utah, Arizona and Mexico. The meeting was held for "many moons" and a set of tenets called "the first laws" was compiled that contained knowledge related to man's development and purpose on the earth.[21]

At some point during this period a sudden earth change occurred so that "the lands disappeared in the low places" in Peru. Many people were killed although some who were living on the higher elevations survived.[22]

200,000 B.C.
The Rise of the Atlantean Civilization

By 200,000 BC there had been "many changes in the surface of what is now called the earth." The "southern portions of South America" as we currently view them were above sea level, but were located nearer to the North Pole. It was at this time that the Atlantean civilization began to establish itself.[23]

The "Rule of Og" in South America

The people of Og are the earliest civilization named in the readings for South America, although their origins are not specifically dated. In one reading we are told of a time period called "the rule of Og...when the laws were being made in now the Peruvian country."[24] It is also stated clearly that the Og were the ancestors of the Ohum who were in turn the forerunners of the Inca in South America. These peoples (the Inca or the Ohum) were said to have "builded the walls across the mountains (in Peru)..."[25] During the time of the Atlantean civilization the Og of Peru experienced "the beginnings of the communications with those of many other lands."[26]

50,722 B.C. — Gathering of the 5 Nations to Exterminate the Large Animals

Sometime shortly before the first of the three cataclysms that impacted Atlantis and Lemuria, representatives from South America (then called Og) attended a special gathering of nations. Led by the Atlanteans, these leaders met to find a way to protect themselves from

These may be the walls referred to in the Cayce readings.
Source: *Handbook of South American Indians* (1949), Bureau of Ethnology, U.S. Gov. Printing Office.

the large animals that were threatening humans in various areas of the world.[27] This group also had the purpose of promoting peace and "brotherly relationships in the experience of man". Those involved were from Atlantis, China (Mongoloid land), India, Egypt, Carpathia, On and Og (Peru), the Himalayas, the Yucatan, the Andes, and the Pyrenees. However problems resulting from their efforts "brought the periods of the first disintegration in that land."[28]

The First Cataclysm

The first destructive earth changes which affected Atlantis occurred in 50,722 B.C. Powerful explosives used in the attempt to exterminate the large animals caused a volcanic chain reaction. The readings also state that this event constituted the first destruction of Mu.[29] Another reading asserts that "ice,…nature, God, changed the poles and the animals were destroyed, though man attempted it in that activity of the meetings."[30]

The Breaking up of Lemuria:
Lemurian Migrations to North America

It is not clear whether this first Atlantean cataclysm caused the final breaking up of Lemuria as a united area, but this appears highly likely since many Lemurian migrations are described as occurring at that time. For example, one reading states specifically that after this first Atlantean cataclysm some Lemurians sought refuge in Arizona and Utah where they "established the cave dwellers, and the use of the metals as a medium of exchange and adornment."[31] Others from Peru migrated to the "Southwestern portion of North America" seeking "freedom of the peoples."[32] Another reading describes this migration as occurring at a time prior to the appearance of the five races (12,000 B.C.), when there were "changes in the earth surface."[33]

A reading given for a period before the time of Ra Ta asserts that Lemurians escaping "the sinking of Mu or Lemuria" migrated and established settlements in portions of Rocky Mountains, Arizona, New Mexico, Nevada and Utah.[34]

At some period before the time of Ra Ta, people of Mu were aware of the impending breaking up of their lands in the Pacific. Some migrated to current Oregon where "still may be seen SOMETHING of the worship as set up…as the totem or the family tree. At that time the ruling structure was matriarchal.[35]

Atlantean Migrations to Og (South America)
After the First Destruction

The readings tell us that the first wave of Atlantean migrations to South America occurred after the destructions of 50,722 B.C.[36] Some of the Atlanteans who migrated to Og taught the native people about the law of one and set up temples and a highly spiritual form of sacrifice that was later perverted by those from Mu (Gobi?) and "by those from the promised land" (the Lost Tribes of Israel?).[37]

Evidence of Atlantean Migrations
May Still Exist in the Andes

During one of the destructions of Atlantis, a group of Atlanteans from an area near the present day east coast of North America migrated to Peru – then called "the land of Oz and Og." Some of them became involved in "hoarding of wealth" including "those mediums of exchange that were not only beautiful in their own selves but as to the light, as to the influence same had upon the minds of others." A 1936 readings states that records of one of them, a princess named Alsia or Amammia, "may be found yet, among the temples in the Andean experience…the storehouse of wealth of the earth – in golds!"[38]

Beginning of the Ohum or Ohlms in South America

Sometime after the first Atlantean settlements had been established in the area of Peru and Ecuador (Og), the Ohum came into the area and conquered them.[39] Another reading states that the Ohums went to war against "the invaders from over the seas" taking captives which they treated cruelly.[40] During this period the "lands disappeared and re-appeared" which weakened nations and groups in Peru.[41] However, at a time when "the earth was divided" the southern portion of Peru became submerged causing the people there to move to higher ground. A ruler and spiritual leader of these people (who most likely were the ancestors of the Ohum) was named Omrui, although he was eventually renamed Mosases.[42]

Atlantean Influence on Ohum Civilization

Atlanteans from "the northern land" brought changes to the Ohum in Peru related to political and religious matters while another group which left Atlantis "just before the upheavals" and "acted with the Ohums."[43]

One of the Atlanteans who migrated to Peru after the first destructions acted as a "priestess to the sons of Ohum" and served to strengthen communication between Peru and Atlantis to such an extent that her efforts assisted many thousands of years later when the Atlanteans migrated to the Yucatan and Central America.[44]

Characteristics of Ohum Society

The readings call the Ohum the first peoples "in the Peruvian forces." A ruler in those first days of the Ohum was named Omrhdji. He "gave the peoples those principles of self-government that have gone to the best rule through many, many ages."[45] Ohum society was organized such that one person was told that he served as a secretary/body guard/counselor to the ruler.[46] The Ohum civilization also contained divisions, which Cayce describes as "cults", "homes " and "estates." There were even people who moved between the divisions to improve relationships between the different groups.[47]

The Ohum were involved with "converting the elements of earth to the use of man" in the form of jewelry and precious stones.[48] During the Ohum rule there was a "Temple of Mu" in which there was the development of sacrificial offerings "of the highest as was received...of the best." The ritual eventually degraded in some way.[49]

28,000 B.C — Second Cataclysm: More Atlantean Migrations to South America

After the second cataclysm Atlantis had been broken up into several islands and soon thereafter began to experience philosophical and political divisions due in part to the introduction of human sacrifice.[50] This conflict increased to the point that some Atlanteans migrated to other lands including Central America and then on to "the Incal land" where at least one of them served as a priest.[51] Another Atlantean immigrant to Peru established certain religious rituals that resulted in the people coming to worship her.[52]

In addition, before the time of Ra Ta and the final Atlantean destruction, Atlanteans who adhered to the Law of One were continuing to stay in communication with those "as from Om (Ohum?), Mu, the hierarchy land in that NOW known as the United States, in that particular portion of Arizona and Nevada that are as a portion of that Brotherhood of those peoples of Mu."[53]

The Fall of the Ohum

As more and more Atlanteans entered South America, they began to use their advanced spiritual powers to set themselves up in positions of political power.[54] As a result, they became increasingly unwelcome among the Ohum[55] and there was a movement to segregate them from the Ohum rule.[56]

Over time the Ohum's higher spiritual values became degraded by the assimilation of Atlantean tendencies for seeking power and material things and "the gratifying of selfish interest."[57] The Atlanteans who had migrated there had brought more of the "MATERIAL things of life as pertaining to court hangings, ritualistic forces...the worship of the sun and the solar forces...offering of human sacrifice..."[58]

The readings describe a second period for the Ohum that was marked by a focus on material things and "earthly splendor"[59] and in the "latter portion of that rule...satisfaction of the desires of the flesh."[60] As a result there was some sort of rebellion among the Ohum during the ending of their rule that "brought destruction...to man's dwelling."[61] This destruction involved a submergence of "the earth's surface through the eruptions as changed the plane of the earth's surface..."[62] which required them to rely on "peoples (Atlanteans?)...who furnished the building of the lands for the sustenance of the peoples."[63]

12,000 B.C. — The Coming of The Five Adamic Races

Approximately 12,000 B.C. the readings tell us that five Adamic races of modern man were projected in five places simultaneously around the world. One of these places was the Peruvian Andes—the location of the projection of the brown race.[64] One reading states that during the period of their last ruler, the Ohum were a peaceful people who resided in the southern portion of Peru. It curiously adds that they were "subdued by the peoples coming in from the place of many waters in the south country from there." These people who took over their rule were called "the developing race" which may refer to the brown Adamic race.[65]

Atlantean Migrations Before the Final Cataclysm

Some Atlanteans migrated to Peru and the Yucatan lands before the final upheavals (10,000 B.C.) primarily in an attempt to escape persecution.[66] They built temples, one of which had just "recently been discovered in that of the southern portion" of either Peru or Yucatan at the time of an October 1931 reading.[67]

One Atlantean was among a group who traveled to "the Central American land or Yucatan" from Peru "the land of the Ohums" to escape "the trembles of the Atlantean land" and to establish "a new kingdom." She became the high priestess of a temple built there.[68]

The Introduction of Atlantean Technology to South America

When the refugees from Poseidea in Atlantis reached Peru they found that the Ohum were involved with "precious stones and precious metals."[69]

Some Atlanteans, aware of the impending destruction of their island, migrated to Peru and brought technology regarding the "application of the electrical forces...and the activities of same upon metals." They used this technology not only to find these metals, but also to transport and refine them. The readings noted that they had the capability to combine iron and copper as was done later in the areas of the Middle East. They were also able to create electrical generators of some sort. Interestingly, the metals they mined were used to create "magnetic forces" that were applied to the physical body in order to regenerate it and for "the transmuting of the bodies in preparation for the new race."[70]

One group of Atlanteans who were involved in planning the migrations brought records from their homeland and customs that would help them to establish a more advanced civilization in Peru, the Yucatan, and North America. These Atlanteans had aircraft and watercraft and were able to communicate with other lands "through the forces of nature."[71]

South American Influences in the Yucatan & Southwest U.S.

Lemurian (Peruvian?) influences are said to have dominated in the Yucatan prior to the final destruction of Atlantis. During that same time period, migrating Atlanteans encountered native peoples of Lemurian and Atlantean descent who had moved north from Peru at some earlier time. These people, along with a remnant of the Lost Tribes of Israel (after 3000 B.C.), were the ancestors of the Maya.[72]

Some of the Peruvians migrating north to the Yucatan met with the Maya and suffered some sort of persecutions. These persecutions involved the establishment of an elite ruling level among the society which looked down upon and made slaves of those outside their group.[73]

Buildings constructed in the Yucatan during this period were a part of a "new activity that became destructive because of the influences from the land of Og and On and the activities that arose in the western portion of that particular period." This included an "upheaval which settled so much in portions of that now known as the southwestern U.S.A."[74]

Some of the descendants of the Atlanteans and "the Inca or the land of Og" who settled in the Yucatan attempted to re-establish "the older portions of the Atlantean civilization" by setting up temples which were" beginning to be uncovered" in 1937.[75]

Peoples who were the descendants of Atlantis and Peru also influenced Temple building in Central America.[76] In fact, one readings states that "the pyramid, the altars before the doors of the varied temple activities" found now in the Yucatan were influenced by the people of Oz who are often mentioned in relation to Og.[77] These buildings may also be connected to a "Temple of Oz" in Atlantis that was used by the materialistic "Sons of Belial" group. It is described as being beautiful on the outside "but temples of sin within."[78] One reading describes a Peruvian princess who led a group to the Yucatan where they built temples for sun worship. The princess served as priestess and was a "taker of blood."[79]

Atlanteans migrating to the Yucatan around the time of the final destruction of Atlantis also communicated with and journeyed to the north and west in order to connect with the descendants of Lemuria in Arizona and those in the Death Valley area of lower California.[80]

There was also interaction and contact between the Ohums of Peru and the groups that went to Yucatan. This brought advancement to the Ohum in the use of "signs of the heavens" for determining crop planting and to predict the activities of man. It also brought the beginnings of degradation caused by "the offering of bodily forces" (blood?) in religious sacrifices.[81]

10,600 B.C. — South America's International Contacts at the Time of Ra Ta of Egypt

Cayce relates that there was frequent contact between South America and other areas of the world in the 10,000-B.C. era. For example a princess of the Atlanteans who was a member of the Law of One moved to Peru to escape "the divisions and the destruction" caused by the Sons of Belial. She remained a princess to her people and continued to experience problems until "associations or communications" were made with people from Egypt.[82]

Before the final destruction of Atlantis, Ra Ta of Egypt gathered representatives from all over the world "for the correlating of the truths." Lands involved included the Nordic land, Mu, Og, Persia, Abyssinia, Mongolia, Caucasia, "that now known as the American land, or the Zu of the Oz," India, Egypt, the Incal, the Pyrenees, the Carpathian land, Atlantis, and the Gobi (Mu?), as well as Indo-China or Siam.[83]

Also during this time, Ra Ta and others traveled around the world spreading the highest spiritual teachings and gathering information about the belief systems of the various groups including "the Incan, and even in what may be called the descendants from Mu or Lemuria."[84]

The readings also describe "storehouses, that would be called banks in the present, or places of exchange" established for the purpose of promoting interaction between Egypt, Poseidia, Og, Pyrenees, Sicily, Norway, China, India, Peru, and other parts of the Americas during time of Ra Ta.[85]

10,400 – 10,000 B.C — The Final Atlantean Destruction and The Rise of the Inca Civilization

Following the time of Ra Ta there were peoples from "other lands" who settled in the" Incal land" of Peru.[86] According to the readings, "the Incal were themselves the successors of those of Oz or Og (Peru), and Mu in the southern portion of that now called California and Mexico and southern New Mexico in the United States."[87]

The readings also note that members of a ruling group in Atlantis called the "house of Inca" migrated to Peru after the final destruction and began the Incal rein over the Ohums.[88] One reading talks about a time "before the Incals and the peoples of the Poseidian land entered."[89]

Characteristics of the First Inca Civilization

The Atlanteans who had migrated to the Incal land in Peru attempted to recreate their previous civilization by educating young people, building homes, creating home conveniences, attending to the weak and disabled, as well as promoting activities such as, basket weaving, bookmaking, rug designing, painting, and song writing.[90] The Inca who ruled at this time were described as being involved with music, art, and braided and beaded works.[91]

During the Incal rule there was much emphasis on mining and building.[92] It was during this time that "the Conduits – through the Mountains" were built for the purpose of drainage.[93]

The readings identify a priest involved in temple worship named Kaat. During this period the Inca "prepared many of the pitfalls in the mountains, where the machineries were prepared for lifting and lowering the precious stones as were gathered." They were also involved with "preparing the waterways for protection and for assistance in gathering such jewels."[94]

In addition, the Inca built many temples around which they created many religious rituals and ceremonies.[95] One person was told she was a priestess in the "Incan or Peruvian land" and that she was segregated and not allowed to have relations with men. She was "surrounded with pomp and with all conveniences."[96] "In the days of the first Incal, as known" draperies used in temples were woven or sewn containing raised "figures on cloth."[97]

3000 BC and Later — Inca Migrations To Alabama and Florida (With Yucatan, & Norse Peoples)

After the time of Moses and the Exodus (in one reading this event is dated at 5500 B.C.), and at the beginning of the Mound Builder period, people from the Yucatan, from Peru, including the Inca, and from the Norse land, settled in the eastern portion of Alabama and Florida. Some of the people present were "of a race of unusual height, unusual proportions to what might be termed in the present." These people were "the lords of the land" and gave instructions to the other peoples regarding moral and religious tenets and in regards to "penal codes."[98]

To Argentina

Sometime between the final destruction of Atlantis and the Christian Crusades of the Middle Ages, the Inca of Peru journeyed to the area of modern-day Argentina thus spreading their sacred teachings to the peoples of other parts of South America.[99]

To Central Ohio becoming Mound Builders

Sometime after 3000 BC there was a migration of a group of people who were the descendents of the Lost Tribes of Israel and people who had lived in Atlantis, Yucatan, Peru (Inca), and the land of On (Og?) to central Ohio becoming the first people to build mounds in that area. The readings tell us that these people "centralized" their sometimes-conflicting belief systems and put much energy into building individual homes and in relating to nature.[100]

Summary

The detail provided in the Cayce readings give us an overview of the many events that transpired in ancient South America as well as occasional glimpses into the lives of these ancient people. South America was a mixture of peoples from many different locations including people from Atlantis and Mu. In addition, Cayce tells us that the oldest people on earth resided in portions of South America that were once considered to be a part of Mu.

Cayce reveals that the people in ancient South America went through numerous times of conflict and religious strife. Once each period of strife ended, it seems as though nature dealt another blow to the inhabitants of South America producing new waves of migrations both in and out of the continent.

In general, much of the Cayce story is supported by the genetic evidence and the archaeological record. We do know that various people migrated to the continent in essentially the same time frames Cayce gave—especially in the periods of 28,000 B.C. and 10,000 B.C. We also have tantalizing hints about technology. For example, the skills of the ancient people in South America in metalworking, masonry, and architectural design were among the very best of the world. We also have the possibility that these ancient people had some knowledge about hot-air balloons.

Chapter 9

Cayce's Chronology of Ancient South America Appears to be Valid

As we stated in the very beginning of this book, we did not intend to provide a comprehensive review of South American archaeology or a complete review of Cayce. What we proposed to do was to review the most recent findings and make a comparison between Cayce's assertions and the current state of the evidence. What has emerged from this effort strongly supports Cayce's readings on the chronology of ancient migrations to the Americas. A brief review of Cayce's major chronological reference points and the current evidence follows.

1. First Humans in Lemuria/South America—10,500,000 B.C.

Presently there is no evidence in support of the claim that humans were in South America in this very remote time. Scientific research has, however, routinely pushed the accepted date of proto-humans' existence back in time. When Cayce made this rather impossible statement, science believed that hominids might have existed for 200,000 years. At this writing, the first known hominids are now dated to as old as 8 million years, but the researchers now openly speculate that they believe the evidence will eventually take this date to 10-11 million years.

In support of Cayce, it should be noted that the climate in both South America and America's Southwest have not been ideal for the long-term preservation of remains. It should also be noted that the only evidence of this ancient occupation of the Americas mentioned in the

Cayce readings is the existence of a few cave paintings. Nevertheless, Cayce's 10,500,000 B.C. date for the first form of human-like creatures looks better and better.

2. The Occupation of South America Prior to 200,000 B.C.

Two published studies in the archaeological literature currently point to humans living in ancient South America and Mexico in this time frame. The dates of these sites (300,000 B.C. and 250,000 B.C.) would support Cayce's contention that parts of South America were occupied in 200,000 B.C. While North American archaeologists argue that the findings are impossible, the fact remains that a team from the U.S. Geological Survey, a French dating lab, and several archaeologists have presented the evidence as reliable and accurate.

3. The Circa 50,000 B.C. Migrations From Atlantis and Mu

Numerous radiocarbon dates have come from a host of South American sites, showing that widespread human occupation of South America occurred around this date. In addition, genetic research points to early migrations to the Americas centering on the date of 47,000 B.C. (quite close to Cayce's 50,000 B.C. date). Genetics-based research attempts to point to the origin of these migrations by finding other areas in the world where large populations of the same genetic types currently live. Thus, if the origin of a migrating group was in a land that no longer exists, this could not be identified. However, the entrance of haplogroups X and B into the Americas almost exactly matches Cayce's chronology of migrations from Mu and Atlantis. The possibility that haplogroup B originated in Mu and haplogroup X originated in Atlantis is completely supported by the current evidence.

4. The Existence of Other People in the Americas

Cayce related that several mysterious groups already lived in the Americas prior to migrations in 28,000 B.C., and that several other groups from other locations migrated here. These people were not from Atlantis or Mu. Further, he related that there were "invaders from over the seas," the Ohum, and sometimes people described as coming from the "West." In addition, he cited that frequent movements between the the American continents occurred. It should be kept in mind that Cayce made these statements at a time archaeologists believed the Americas had been occupied for only a few thousand years. The presence of haplogroups A, B, C, D, X, and newly discovered—but as-yet unidentified—haplogroups in South America basically supports Cayce's ideas.

5. The Migration of People From Mu to America's Southwest

The Cayce readings specifically mention the migration of a large group of people from South America to America's Southwest. He calls this area a portion of "the Brotherhood of those peoples of Mu." The near-exclusive concentration of haplogroup B in America's Southwest —and its high concentration on South America's Pacific side—strongly supports Cayce's statements and also points to haplogroup B as originating in Mu. In fact, haplogroup B is now known to have entered the Southwest several times—matching Cayce's chronology. The new genetic research on the Oceanic-Speaking Peoples strongly suggests that they have an extremely old origin in their present homeland. Finally, Cayce related that in 28,000 B.C. Mu experienced a severe physical disruption, causing many people to seek safer lands. The known movement of people into Melanesia in 28,000 B.C. strongly supports Cayce's chronology of the events in this time frame.

6. The 28,000 B.C. Migrations From Atlantis and Mu

In 28,000 B.C., the Cayce readings reveal migrations to North and South America came from both Mu and Atlantis. The 28,000 B.C. date is frequently turning up in archaeological speculations and in genetic research and is now basically accepted as one of the dates of major migrations into the Americas. The entrance of haplogroup X and B into the Americas in this time frame also fully supports Cayce.

7. The 10,000 B.C. Migrations From Atlantis

Cayce related that Atlanteans went to locations in North, Central, and South America just before 10,000 B.C. In addition, Atlanteans migrated to other areas of the world well before 10,000 B.C. These areas include the Pyrenees Mountains, Israel, Egypt, and the Gobi area. The existence of haplogroup X in ancient remains found in each and every one of these locations is very suggestive. In addition, the similarity of America's Clovis culture to Europe's earlier Solutrean culture completely fits Cayce's chronology. As stated earlier, the idea that a now-lost civilization located between America and Europe was the source of haplogroup X and the Clovis and Solutrean cultures seems far more reasonable than recent speculations about an ice-bridge migration.

8. Technology in Ancient South America

The Cayce readings reveal that manipulating and controlling the magnetic properties of various stones and metals was a technological ability taken to South America by Atlanteans. Cayce also stated that some form of system was developed to produce electrical energies to apply to metals. It is recognized that sophisticated metalworking ability was present in South America, and that certain types of stones—especially magnetic stones—were seen as having an almost magical healing quality. *The Lost Hall of Records* details quite a few of the speculations and possibilities on the use of magnetized stones in Central America. *Mound Builders* presents evidence that specific forms of ritual utilizing magnetic fields were employed in healing and spiritual ceremonies.

Evidence supporting the possibility that a system to produce electrical energy was present in ancient South America does not—to our knowledge—exist. On the other hand, Cayce's assertion that hot-air balloon technology was present in ancient South America is certainly possible if not highly probable. Cayce was once asked how emissaries had traveled to meetings involving representatives of the entire world (reading 953-24). He replied, "Lighter than air...as would today be termed balloons." Some South American myths and legends can be interpreted as involving balloons, and the observations that tribes in various locations knew how to make, fill, and release smoke balloons supports the idea. Finally, the extensive research and actual demonstration of how the ancients could have launched a primitive hot-air balloon at Nazca (by the Explorers' group) fully supports this aspect of the Cayce readings.

9. The Origin of the Inca

Traditional archaeology is uncertain about the origin of the Inca. What is known is that by the time the Spanish entered South America, the population of the Inca elite was 40,000 and their subjects numbered over 10 million. The Inca began in the Cuzco area, and it is believed that a small number of individuals were involved in their beginning, just as the legends relate. The Cayce readings tell us that just before

10,000 B.C. there were people from "other lands" who were already living in the areas where the Inca Empire was established. Not long after 10,000 B.C., a small group of individuals who were members of the ruling class of Atlantis—and also apparently related to each other—went to Peru. According to Cayce, these people were from the Atlantean "House of Inca." It was from this migration that the Inca Empire eventually developed.

Haplogroup X—what we have hypothesized as Atlantean mtDNA—has been found in some ancient burials in the Andes and in other places that were once in the Inca Empire. It may be that ancient remains of individuals who were known to be members of the Inca elite will eventually be tested. But for the moment, all we can say with certainty is that haplogroup X was present in the Andes in the time frame given in the Cayce readings. Cayce's story falls in line with the legends and myths revealing the mysterious origin of the Inca, and the combined weight of these facts tends to support Cayce.

10. Post-3000 B.C. Migrations

In *Mound Builders* we described a 3000 B.C. migration to America by a group Cayce called "remnants of Lost Tribes." In 1997 the location of this group's first habitation site in America may have been found. It was at Watson Brake, Louisiana where a 22-acre, circular enclosure was made, with 11 mounds erected on the earthen enclosure. According to Cayce, this group later migrated to the Mexico City area. Interestingly, the people who built Watson Brake inhabited the site less than 180 years and then they simply disappeared. We speculate that these people were Cayce's "Lost Tribes," and that they did, in fact, migrate to the Mexico City area between perhaps 2800 B.C. and 3000 B.C.

Cayce then relates that the descendants of these Lost Tribes (in Mexico) joined with the descendants of the Atlanteans living in the Yucatan. In order to escape the increasing human sacrifice practices, this larger group then moved to America, where they established mound building. The first mound site of this group appears to have been only 40 miles from Watson Brake, at what is today known as Poverty Point. Carbon dating at Poverty Point shows that someone entered the site (probably coming up the Mississippi River) in perhaps 2000 B.C.

The Cayce readings then explain that this group of Atlanteans and Lost Tribes gradually moved up the Mississippi River and into the

Ohio River Valleys. There they established the sophisticated mound building cultures found in Eastern America. In fact, the most recent archaeological explanation is that a series of movements came from the south, up the Mississippi River, resulting in the establishment of the mound builder culture.

It is important to recall that Cayce placed Atlanteans and their descendants in the Iroquois lands (including the Ohio area) in 10,000 B.C. Thus, according to Cayce, the Atlanteans migrating from the south *circa* 1000 B.C. merged with Atlantean descendants who had long been in that region. As discussed in the genetics chapter, a most remarkable piece of evidence has emerged which supports the contention that Atlanteans came into the area in 1000 B.C., joining Atlanteans who were already present. Evidence shows that people bearing haplogroup X were living in the Iroquois lands by 10,000 B.C. But sometime around 1000 B.C., a new group of people bearing haplogroup X entered the area.

Summary & Conclusions

Our brief comparison of Cayce's claims with the findings from current archaeological and genetic research heavily weighs in Cayce's favor. In fact, each and every one of the major ideas expressed in the Cayce readings about ancient South America, Mu, and Atlantis have substantial support from both archaeological findings and genetics. Whether or not this pattern will continue remains to be seen, but as our view of the ancient world becomes more and more clear, Cayce looks better and better. At the same time, the more we learn from modern genetic research and the release of previously suppressed excavation findings, the worse mainstream archaeology looks. For 70 years we have been told that the Americas were devoid of human life prior to 9500 B.C. We were told that these ancient people could not possibly cross the oceans. We were told that everyone who entered ancient America came from Siberia. We were told that the people of ancient America had no contact with the "outside world" until 1492. Each and every one of these closely guarded, cherished ideas in mainstream American archaeology—the "holy writ," as some disagreeing archaeologists has called them—have now been shown to be completely false.

Hundreds of books have been written on Atlantis and Mu, and the topics hold intense public interest. Television documentaries on Atlantis continue to be popular, and radio talk shows such as Art Bell's "Dreamland" focus on Atlantis routinely. What can account for such interest?

Speculations from archaeologists cite a gullible public as a major explanation for the popularity of "false beliefs" such as Atlantis. In addition, they attribute a host of rather undesirable motivations to people who continue to write about and research Atlantis. According to this idea, anyone who speculates that Atlantis may actually have existed is a pseudoarchaeologist who lies on the lunatic fringe. In *Fantastic Archaeology*,[1] Williams quotes a colleague who describes the continuing fascination of the public on such taboo topics as Atlantis rather harshly: "Too many people lurk in the lush lunatic fringes around the fairway of true archaeology."

Williams relates that a number of archaeologists have strongly felt that a major responsibility of professionals in their field is to "prevent pseudoarchaeologists from robbing humanity of the real achievements of past cultures." Taking this sentiment to heart, archaeology college students quickly learn in a popular textbook the academic mainstream truth about Atlantis—"It simply did not exist."[2] But could this statement itself be robbing humanity of the achievements of past cultures?

A great deal of psychological research has been conducted on the topic of beliefs and why people will believe in things that are unsupported by science. This research does not cite lunacy as a factor, and gullibility is found in everyone—including scientists. Archaeologists are themselves engaging in pseudoscience when they attempt to employ psychological terms to try to explain why a vast proportion of the population disagrees with their blanket statements they make as indisputable facts. In addition, it appears that the long held beliefs in mainstream archaeology were held together by pseudoscience operating at the worst level—within what purports to be science.

Pseudoscience is well defined in the scientific literature, and it has several primary characteristics. These are: a hostility to criticism; claims of conspiracy; the use of single cases to "prove a point;" the use of simplistic solutions to explain complex findings; the utilization of meaningless terms cloaked in scientific language; the use of bold, inflammatory statements to deride the opposition; attempts to shift the burden of proof; and making unsubstantiated claims.[3]

In our series of books investigating the chronology of the ancient world as revealed in the Edgar Cayce readings, we have endeavored to follow the evidence wherever it leads. We have presented the most up-to-date evidence available and utilized scientific terms within the context of their accepted meanings. We have tried to include all of the exidence and do not believe that a conspiracy is present to keep us from the truth. In contrast, the mainstream archaeological community shows increasing hostility to outsiders and frequently derides those "on the lunatic fringe" who suggest that the accepted views are wrong or incomplete. But the core issue should not involve arguments about pseudoscience. The core issue is truth. Let the facts fall where they will.

The Cayce readings on ancient history may eventually prove to be valid, partly valid, or completely false. Presently, the weight of evidence falls heavily on the side of Cayce. But the most important issue revealed in Cayce's readings does not relate to the existence of Atlantis or Mu. Nor does it relate to a hall of records or a pattern of ancient migrations. The most important issue discussed in the Cayce readings relates to the spiritual nature of humankind and our connection to something far greater than ourselves. The manner in which we conduct our lives and the ways in which we impact others who are on this path of life with us is what truly matters. For some people, the confirmation of Atlantis is a way of validating the existence of a spiritual side to humanity. It may be that some who are on this quest may *want* Atlantis to someday be confirmed, because the alternative is viewed as bleak. Conversely, those who are so strident in denying Atlantis may well *want* it to eventually be disproved, because the alternative is too disturbing.

Chapter References

Chapter 1

[1] Salzano, F. M., & Bortolini, M. C. (2002) *The evolution and genetics of Latin American Populations.* NY: Cambridge Univ. Press.

[2] Politis, G. G., & Alberti, B. (1999) *Archaeology in Latin America.* NY: Routledge.

[3] Williams, S. (1991) *Fantastic Archaeology.* Philadelphia: Univ. of PA Press.

[4] Lewis, R. B. (Ed.) (1996) *Kentucky Archaeology.* Lexington: Univ. of KY Press.

[5] *The World Atlas of Archaeology* (1985) English edition: NY: Portland House.

[6] Little, G. L., Van Auken, J., & Little, L. (2001) *Mound Builders.* Memphis, TN: Eagle Wing Books.

[7] Reading 2665-2.

[8] Thompson, J. A. (1922) *The Outline of Science.* NY: Putnam.

[9] Van Auken, J., & Little, L. (2000) *Lost Hall of Records.* Mem., TN: Eagle Wing Bks.

Chapter 2

[1] Politis, G. G., & Alberti, B. (1999) *Archaeology in Latin America.* NY: Routledge.

[2] *Radiocarbon Database for the Andes, Chronological index. (Older than 12000 conv. BP)* www.uw.edu.pl/uw/andy/CHR0012.HTM.

[3] Bryan, A. L. (2002) The original peopling of Latin America. Chapter in T. R. Rabiela & J. V. Murra (Eds.) *Las sociedades originarias (The Indigenous Societies)* Mexico: Historia General de America Latina.

[4] Discoveries in Brasilia Untie Archaeological Debate. *Actualidades Arqueloógicas*, Vol. 22, April-June, 2000.

[5] Steward, J. H. (Ed.) *Handbook of South American Indians.* 5 vols. (1946, 1946, 1948, 1949, 1950) Bureau of Am. Ethnology. Washington, DC: U.S. Gov. Printing Office.

Chapter 3

[1] Lumbreras, L. (1974) *The Peoples and Cultures of Ancient Peru.* Washington, D.C.: Smithsonian Institution Press.

[2] Moseley, M. (1993) *The Incas and Their Ancestry.* London: Thames and Hudson.

[3] MacNeish, R., Bradley, V., Nelken-Terner, A. & Phagan, C. (1980) *Prehistory of the Ayacucho Basin, Peru.* Ann Arbor: University of Michigan Press.

[4] Jennings, J. D., & Rick, J. W. (1980) *Prehistoric Hunters of the High Andes.* Ac. Pr.

[5] Von Hagan, A., & Morris, C. (1998) *The Cities of the Ancient Andes.* London: Thames and Hudson.

[6] Burger, R. L. (1992) *Chavin and the origins of Andean civilization.* London: Thames and Hudson.

[7] Shinoda, K., Shimada, I., Alva, W., & Uceda, S. (2002) DNA analysis of Moche and Sicán populations: Results and implications. Paper presented at Archaeology of the Paleoindians, March 21, 2002.

Chapter 4

[1] Little, G. L. (1997) *Psychopharmacology: Basics for counselors.* Memphis: ATA.

[2] Milnor, J, P., & Little, G. L. (2000) *It Can Break Your Heart.* Mem.: Eagle Wing Books.

[3] Shimada, I., Shinoda, K., Bourget, S., Alva, W., & Uceda, S. (2002) mtDNA analysis of Mochia and Sicán populations of Pre-Hispanic Peru. In: *Proceedings of the April 2002 Biomolecular Conference.* Carbondale, IL: Center for Archaeological Excavations.

[4] Alves-Silva, J., Santos, M., *et. al.* (2000) The ancestry of Brazilian mtDNA Lineages. *American Journal of Human Genetics,* 67, 444-461.

[5] Malhi, R. S., et. al. (2002) The structure of diversity within New World mitochondrial DNA haplogroups: Implications for the prehistory of North America. *American Journal of Human Genetics,* 70.

[6] Bert, F., Corella, A., *et. al.* (2001) Major mitochondrial haplogroup heterogeneity in Highland and Lowland Amerindian populations from Bolivia. *Human Biology,* 73 (1).

[7] Starikovskaya, Y., & Sukernik, R. I., *et. al.* (1998) *American Journal of Human Genetics,* 63, 1473-1491.

[8] Hurles, M. E., Nicholson, J., Bosch, E., Renfrew, C., *et. al.* (2002) Y chromosomal evidence for the origins of the Oceanic-Speaking Peoples. *Genetics,* 160, 289-303.

Chapter 6

[1] Woodman, J. (1977) *Nazca: Journey to the Sun.* NY: Simon & Schuster.

[2] Childress, D.H. (1986) *Lost Cities & Ancient Mysteries of South America.* Kempton, IL: Adventures Unlimited Press.

Chapter -7

[1] Readings 364 and 5748 series.

[2] Reading 364-13.
[3] Cayce, Edgar E., Schwartzer, Gail Cayce, and Richards, Douglas G. (1997) *Mysteries of Atlantis Revisited.* New York: St. Martins Paperback's.
[4] Church, W. H. (1989) *Edgar Cayce's Story of the Soul.* Virginia Beach: A.R.E. Press.
[5] Carlson, Vada F. (1970) *The Great Migration: Prehistory and the Edgar Cayce Readings.* Virginia Beach: A.R.E. Press.
[6] Readings 5748-1, 5748-2.
[7] Reading 364-4.
[8] Reading 851-2.
[9] Reading 470-22.
[10] Cayce, Edgar E., Schwartzer, Gail Cayce, and Richards, Douglas G. (1997) *Mysteries of Atlantis Revisited.* New York: St. Martins Paperback's, p. 54.
[11] Readings 364-7, 364-13.
[12] Church, W. H. (1989) *Edgar Cayce's Story of the Soul.* Virginia Beach: A.R.E. Press, p. 110.
[13] Church, W.H. (1995) *The Lives of Edgar Cayce.* Virginia Beach: A.R.E. Press.
[14] Zeilik, M. (1985) *Astronomy.* NY: Harper-Row.
[15] Readings 436-2, 2906-1, 364 series.
[16] Reading 1387-1.
[17] Reading 364-13.
[18] Reading 2665-2.
[19] Reading 364-4.
[20] Reading 877-10.
[21] Readings 5748-1, 5748-2.
[22] Readings 182-2.
[23] Reading 364-4.
[24] Reading 2656-1.
[25] Reading 364-4.
[26] Reading 1226-1.
[27] Reading 262-39.
[28] Reading 1938-2.
[29] Reading 3188-1.
[30] Reading 5249-1.
[31] Reading 816-3.
[32] Reading 2667-5.
[33] Reading 1179-1.
[34] Reading 851-2.
[35] Reading 630-21.
[36] Readings 2829-1 3042-1.
[37] Reading 442-1.
[38] Reading 1183-1.
[39] Reading 99-6).
[40] Reading 427-3.
[41] Reading 2365-2.
[42] Reading 470-2.
[43] Reading 491-1.
[44] Reading 832-1.
[45] Reading 2801-5.
[46] Reading 2904-1.
[47] Reading 2364-1.
[48] Reading 2731-1.
[49] Reading 2698-1.
[50] Readings 364-4, 1101-1.
[51] Reading 670-1.
[52] Reading 3285-2.
[53] Reading 812-1.
[54] Reading 2686-1.
[55] Readings 404-1, 949-2.
[56] Reading 1716-1.
[57] Readings 960-4, 760-4, 1916-5, 1909-1.
[58] Reading 2887-1.
[59] Reading 228-2.
[60] Reading 2895-1.
[61] Reading 5540-5.
[62] Reading 265-2.
[63] Reading 2903-1.
[64] Reading 364-9.
[65] Reading 4713-1.
[66] Reading 5252-1.
[67] Reading 2141-1.
[68] Reading 1730-1.
[69] Reading 488-5.
[70] Reading 470-22.
[71] Reading 1215-4.
[72] Reading 5750-1.
[73] Reading 1637-1.
[74] Reading 1604-1.
[75] Reading 1437-1.
[76] Readings 826-2, 845-1.
[77] Readings 1183-1, 5750-1.
[78] Reading 436-2.
[79] Reading 772-2.
[80] Readings 1434-1, 1473-1.
[81] Reading 1895-1.
[82] Reading 5257-1.
[83] Readings 1648-1, 1387-1, 818-1, 980-1, 987-2, 1650-1, 1397-1 1604-1.
[84] Readings 876-1, 1438-1, 815-2.
[85] Reading 294-148.
[86] Reading 2437-1.
[87] Reading 5750-1.
[88] Readings 3611-1, 3345-1.
[89] Reading 1916-5.
[90] Reading 2988-2.
[91] Reading 2486-1.
[92] Reading 2460-1.
[93] Reading 2888-2.
[94] Reading 1005-2.
[95] Reading 1725-1.
[96] Reading 2454-3.
[97] Reading 4805-1.
[98] Reading 1298-1.
[99] Reading 2281-1.
[100] Reading 1286-1.

Chapter 9
[1] Williams, S. (1991) *Fantastic Archaeology.* Philadelphia: Univ. of PA Press.
[2] Feder, K. L. (1990) *Frauds, Myths, and Mysteries.* Mountain View, CA: Mayfield Pub. Co.
[3] *The New England Skeptical Society's Encyclopedia of Skepticism and the Paranormal.* www.theness.com/encyc/pseudosciencesandbeliefsystems-encyc.html

Index